ethical space

The International Journal of Communication Ethics

Publishing Office
Abramis Academic
ASK House
Northgate Avenue
Bury St. Edmunds
Suffolk
IP32 6BB
UK

Tel: +44 (0)1284 717884
Fax: +44 (0)1284 717889
Email: info@abramis.co.uk
Web: www.abramis.co.uk

Copyright
All rights reserved. No part of this publication may be reproduced in any material form (including photocopying or storing it in any medium by electronic means, and whether or not transiently or incidentally to some other use of this publication) without the written permission of the copyright owner, except in accordance with the provisions of the Copyright, Designs and Patents Act 1988, or under terms of a licence issued by the Copyright Licensing Agency Ltd, 33-34, Alfred Place, London WC1E 7DP, UK. Applications for the copyright owner's permission to reproduce part of this publication should be addressed to the Publishers.

Back issues
Back issues are available from the Publishers at the above editorial address.

© 2022 Abramis Academic

ISSN 1742-0105
ISBN 978-1-84549-801-6

Aims and scope

The commitment of the academic quarterly, *Ethical Space*, is to examine significant historical and emerging ethical issues in communication. Its guiding principles are:

- internationalism,
- independent integrity,
- respect for difference and diversity,
- interdisciplinarity,
- theoretical rigour,
- practitioner focus.

In an editorial in Vol. 3, Nos 2 and 3 of 2006, the joint editor, Donald Matheson, of Canterbury University, New Zealand, stresses that ethics can be defined narrowly, as a matter of duty or responsibility, or ethics can be defined broadly 'blurring into areas such as politics and social criticism'. *Ethical Space* stands essentially at the blurred end of the definitional range. Dr Matheson observes: 'As many commentators have pointed out, a discussion of ethics that is divorced from politics is immediately unable to talk about some of the most important factors in shaping communication and media practices.'

The journal, then, aims to provide a meeting point for media experts, scholars and practitioners who come from different disciplines. Moreover, one of its major strands is to problematise professionalism (for instance, by focusing on alternative, progressive media) and highlight many of its underlying myths.

Submissions

Papers should be submitted to the Editor via email. Full details on submission – along with detailed notes for authors – are available online:
www.ethical-space.co.uk

Subscription Information

Each volume contains 4 issues, issued quarterly. Enquiries regarding subscriptions and orders, both in the UK and overseas, should be sent to:

Journals Fulfilment Department
Abramis Academic, ASK House, Northgate Avenue, Bury St. Edmunds, Suffolk IP32 6BB, UK.
Tel: +44 (0)1284 717884, Fax: +44 (0)1284 717889
Email: info@abramis.co.uk

Your usual subscription agency will also be able to take a subscription to *Ethical Space*.

For the current annual subscription costs please see the subscription information page at the back of this issue.

www.ethical-space.co.uk

ethical space

The International Journal of Communication Ethics

Contents

Special issue in honour of Brian Winston

Editorial

'The transformative academic' – by Richard Lance Keeble — Page 2

Papers

Humans as cultural beings in theory and practice – by Clifford G. Christians — Page 6

How the UK government threatens to impose online censorship – by Julian Petley — Page 16

Towards restorative narrative – by Pratāp Rughani — Page 25

Tributes

'Praxis personified: He did not just talk media, he made it' – by John Mair — Page 32

'Proud, paid-up member of the awkward squad' – by Ivor Gaber — Page 33

Book reviews

Florian Zollmann on *The roots of fake news: Objecting to objectivity*, by Brian Winston and Matthew Winston, and Stephen J. A. Ward on *It's the media, stupid! Essays in honour of Brian Winston*, edited by Richard Lance Keeble — Page 35

Plus

Paper

The sound of silence: European news coverage of refugees in Greece and what is left unreported – by Nanna Vedel-Hertz and Allaina Kilby — Page 41

Book reviews

Tom Cooper on *Handbook of global media ethics*, Vols 1 and 2, edited by Stephen J. A. Ward; John Mair on *Fall: The mystery of Robert Maxwell*, by John Preston; Annmaree Watharow on *Many different kinds of love – A story of life, death and the NHS*, by Michael Rosen, and *Every deep-drawn breath: A critical care doctor on healing, recovery, and transforming medicine in the ICU*, by Wes Ely, and Archana Kumari on *The Routledge companion to journalism ethics*, edited by Lada Trifonova Price, Karen Sanders and Wendy N. Wyatt — Page 50

Editorial Board

Joint Editors
Donald Matheson — University of Canterbury, New Zealand
Sue Joseph — University of South Australia
Tom Bradshaw — University of Gloucestershire

Emeritus Editor
Richard Lance Keeble — University of Lincoln

Reviews Editors
Sue Joseph — University of South Australia
David Baines — Newcastle University

Editorial board members
Raphael Alvira — University of Navarra
Mona Baker — Manchester University
Jay Black — Founding editor, Journal of Mass Media Ethics
Shannon Bowen — University of South Carolina
Antonio Castillo — RMIT University, Melbourne
Saviour Chircop — University of Malta
Clifford Christians — University of Illinois-Urbana, USA
Raphael Cohen–Almagor — University of Hull
Tom Cooper — Emerson College, Boston, MA
Roger Domeneghetti — Northumbria University
Deni Elliott — University of Montana
Chris Frost — Liverpool John Moores University
Theodore L. Glasser — Stanford University
Paul Jackson — Manchester Business School
Mike Jempson — Hon. Director, MediaWise Trust
Cheris Kramarae — University of Oregon; Centre for the Study of Women in Society
Takeshi Maezawa — Former Yomiuri ombudsman, scholar/writer
John Mair — Book editor
Ian Mayes — Former *Guardian* Readers' Editor
Jolyon Mitchell — University of Edinburgh
Colleen Murrell — Dublin City University
Kaarle Nordenstreng — Tampere University
Manuel Parez i Maicas — Universitat Autonoma de Barcelona
Ian Richards — University of South Australia, Adelaide
Simon Rogerson — De Montfort University
Lorna Roth — Concordia University, Montreal
Karen Sanders — St Mary's University
John Steel — University of Derby
Ben Stubbs — University of South Australia
Miklos Sukosd — Central European University, Budapest
Barbara Thomass — Ruhruniversität Bochum
Terry Threadgold — Centre for Journalism Studies, Cardiff University
Stephen J. Ward — University of British Columbia
James Winter — University of Windsor, Canada

EDITORIAL

Richard Lance Keeble

The 'transformative academic'

This special issue of *Ethical Space* is dedicated to the memory of Brian Winston, the first chair of the Institute of Communication Ethics, the original publishers of *ES*, who has died aged 80 following a fall.

For half a century Brian wrote on television news, documentaries, freedom of expression and journalism ethics. He presented his ideas with great energy and often provocatively, moving on from work in TV to a number of prominent university posts in the US and UK. An inspirational and extraordinarily committed teacher, just months before he died he presented a talk to a conference of the Association for Journalism Education via Zoom from his hospital bed.

Professor David Chiddick, former Vice-Chancellor of the University of Lincoln, said: 'Brian helped turn shibboleths of traditional universities on their head' and described him as 'a generous, inclusive, empowering and transformative' academic.

The many sides of Brian

In one of his many profiles of Orson Welles, the great theatre critic Kenneth Tynan tells this story: Welles is invited to give a lecture in a small, mid-Western town but very few people turn up and there is no-one to introduce him. So Welles decides to introduce himself. 'Ladies and gentlemen,' he begins, 'I will tell you the highlights of my life. I am a director of plays. I am a producer of plays. I am an actor on the legitimate stage. I am a writer of motion pictures. I write, direct and act on the radio. I am a magician. I also paint and sketch. I am a book publisher. I am a violinist and a pianist.' 'Isn't it strange,' he ends, 'that there are so many of me – and so few of you!'

Like Orson Welles, there were so many Brian Winstons. There was Brian the polymath; the conversationalist and story-teller; the expert on media theory, documentaries, journalism ethics, freedom of expression, media technologies and their histories; the distinguished winner of the US Emmy in 1985; the enormously energetic and often provocative speaker at conferences around the world; author, editor and co-author of 20 major books, the last one, on fake news, written with his son, Matthew; the author of more than 50 book chapters and almost as many journal articles; the winner of a range of prestigious awards for his writings on media technologies, freedom of expression and for increasing the understanding of human rights. And there was Brian the bon viveur; the journalist; the controversialist regularly writing to newspapers with his views; the loyal friend to many; the dedicated father and grandfather.

Brian was very fond of telling a particular joke. Every morning during his trans-Atlantic voyage, an eastern European Jewish immigrant arrives at his breakfast table to be greeted by his companion, a Frenchman, with the phrase:

The inspirational teacher: Brian Winston in dialogue with students

'Bon appetit.' On the first morning, somewhat surprised, the immigrant replies courteously: 'Goldberg,' shakes the hand of his companion and sits down. On the third day of the voyage the mistake is pointed out to him. So on the fourth day he arrives primed. Before the Frenchman can speak, Goldberg utters a loud and cordial: 'Bon appetit,' to which the Frenchman replies urbanely: 'Goldberg.'

The search for understanding

Brian told me that most Jewish jokes are based on such misunderstandings. And in a way, Brian's career as an academic and teacher sought – at root – to replace misunderstanding with understanding. Significantly, the joke appears on the very first page of his first published text, The image of the media (1973) following a quote from a Joni Mitchell song: 'They've paved Paradise and put up a parking lot' – his writings bursting with eclectic cultural references like this.

After studying law at Merton College, Oxford (and remaining a devoted and active alumnus ever since), Brian began a two-year stint as a researcher for Granada TV's World in Action in 1963. Then, from 1965 to 1971, he worked as a producer/director for a range of programmes on the BBC and Granada.

As an academic, his career started in 1971 as media course director at Alvescot College, Oxfordshire or as the blurb for The image of the media put it: 'Too old at thirty for the hectic and glamorous life of a TV producer, he retired to darkest Oxfordshire to put nearly a decade of practical experience and thought into print.'

Since then his posts included research director in the Sociology Department, University of Glasgow. From this came the seminal texts, Bad news (1976) and More bad news (1980), which challenged head-on the commonly held view that television news in Britain, on whatever channel, is more neutral, objective and trustworthy than press coverage. Not surprisingly, the BBC, its halo punctured, was hostile even before publication, threatening the group with the possibility of copyright action, protesting to the university's Principal and putting pressure on the Social Science Research Council to limit the freedom of the researchers.

In 1976, Brian moved to America to be Visiting Adjunct Professor at New York University. Prominent positions followed – at Pennsylvania State University, Cardiff University and the University of Westminster.

In Misunderstanding media (1986), Brian takes the maverick role in which he so often delighted, challenging the widely-trumpeted notions around the 'information revolution'. To support his argument, he formulates a 'law' of the suppression of radical potential suggesting that new telecommunication technologies are introduced only insofar as their disruptive potential is contained.

He develops his ideas relating to the 'invention' of the cinema in Technologies of seeing: Photography, cinematography and television (1996) where he highlights the need for 'thick' rather than monocausal explanations – with the primacy of society as the main agent in setting technology's agenda.

In Media, technology and society (1998), he returns to his notions challenging the concept of the 'information revolution' taking in the complex histories of the telegraph, the telephone, television, calculators, computers, microcomputers, broadcasting networks, communications satellites, cable television and the internet.

In Messages: Free expression, media and the West from Gutenberg to Google (2005), he stresses the media's importance as an essential driver of free expression which underpins all human rights.

Two of his books, A right to offend (2012) and The Rushdie Fatwa and after: A lesson to the circumspect (2014), tackle the issues surrounding the Satanic verses controversy. He concludes: 'The right to free speech and the right within it to offend, because without it we have no free speech, must be maintained. At whatever cost.'

The Act of documenting: Documentary film in the 21st century (2017), written in collaboration with Gail Vanstone and Wang Chi, considers the complex issues relating to audience reception and challenges the essential Eurocentrism of the dominant debate. While his last book, The roots of fake news: Objecting to objectivity (2021), written with his son, Matthew, a teacher in the School of Media, Communication and Sociology at the University of Leicester, elevates the fake news debate to a completely new, high level, taking in its historical, philosophical, legalistic, scientific and ethical dimensions.

Retiring only very recently, he was one of the longest-serving academic staff member at the University of Lincoln, joining in 2002 and serving for periods as Dean of the Faculty of Media and Humanities and Pro-Vice Chancellor. In 2007, he was awarded the university's highest academic post being named The Lincoln Professor.

I first met Brian (who had a fiery temperament) in the 1990s at meetings on the continent of the European Journalism Training Association where he was a charismatic leading voice. Since then I worked with him on a wide range of educational and publishing projects – and it was he who appointed me professor at the University of Lincoln in 2003. I owe him such a lot.

It's the media, stupid!

Just before Brian died, *It's the media, stupid!*, a collection of essays I edited in his honour, was published by Abramis. Luckily, he was able to read through the final PDF. Three chapters from that *festschrift* are carried here. The first, 'Humans as cultural beings in theory and practice', is by Clifford Christians, one of the world leaders in communication ethics who has long been closely associated with *Ethical Space*.

Christians bases his essay on the notion that humans, as the one living species constituted by language, are therefore fundamentally cultural. According to Christians's philosophy-of-the-human, humans know themselves through their symbolic expressions. 'Communication is the creative process of building and affirming the human order though symbols, with cultures the human habitat that results. ... When humans are defined as cultural beings, human affairs are fundamentally interpretive, rather than a matter of scientific explanation presuming neutrality. Since humanity is embedded in an existing cultural world, its sense of being is necessarily historical.'

In this philosophical context, theories are not to be seen as scholastic paradigms of mathematical precision; rather, they tap into the imaginative power that gives an inside perspective on reality. From here, the essay moves on to consider Habermas and critical inquiry, the ideology of instrumentalism, Harold Innis's notion of the 'monopoly of knowledge', perspectivism, Clifford Geertz's stress on 'thick description' (replacing the thinness of statistically precise objectivism) – and much more.

Christians ends with a wonderful celebration of Brian Winston who 'exemplifies the humanities perspective of this essay. As a world class critical theorist, his hermeneutical depth on mediated symbolic systems demonstrates how interpretive scholarship ought to be done in a global era of cross-cultural complexity'.

Questions relating to harm, offence, insult, free expression, censorship, broadcasting regulation and journalistic codes of conduct were at the heart of many of Brian Winston's writings. Julian Petley, in a paper titled, 'Doing harm: How the UK government threatens to impose online censorship', focuses on the notion of harm, deriving from John Stuart Mill, that Brian Winston employs to indicate where the limits of freedom of expression should lie. According to Winston, claims relating to offence and insult have increasingly expanded definitions of harm and, in the process, narrowed the bounds of freedom of expression. Building on these ideas, Petley examines the regime of online regulation currently proposed by the UK government in the form of the Online Safety Bill. This 'threatens to create an unwieldy, unaccountable and unnecessary state apparatus of online censorship, operates with far too broad and vague a notion of harm, and will see material expelled from the online world which is entirely legal in the offline world'.

Across thirty years as a broadcast journalist, Pratāp Rughani has reported on people facing conflict, atrocity or their aftermaths. In South Africa, Rwanda, Aboriginal Australia, the UK and elsewhere he has conceived his documentary filmmaking 'as a kind of arena in which many experiences can unfold, with enough open space for an audience to make sense of competing perceptions and experiences and settle on their own view'. In the final paper drawn from the *festschrift*, 'Towards restorative narrative', Rughani calls for the creation of 'a more relational media – socially designed and biased enough to nurture the connective tissue between communities, drawing on practices from restorative justice including deep listening and searching for shades of grey'. Rughani tells of his experience shooting the documentary *Justine* (2013), about a young woman who rarely speaks and reports enthusiastically on the techniques of the pioneering Vietnamese video artist, Trinh T. Minh-ha, who describes her aspiration in moving image practice as 'restoring proximity of the subject and recognising the place of subjectivity'.

Rughani closes his essay on an important questioning note: 'Can a story production process now emerge that re-conceives media as ethically responsible "connective tissue" to configure a public space to enable storytellers, subjects and audiences to understand and relate to their diverging perspectives?'

Other chapters in *It's the media, stupid!* include Tom Waugh on 'The documentaries of Magnus Isacsson (1948-2012)', Deane Williams on 'Naïve realism: Repositioning Kracauer's theory', Kate Nash on 'Covid-19 conspiracy documentary: Claiming the real in a context of uncertainty', Annette Hill on 'The act of watching documentary', Raphael Cohen-Almagor on 'The price of ridiculing the prophet: The *Charlie Hebdo* affair', Ivor Gaber on 'Fake news, double spin and strategic lying in the post-truth era' and Martin Conboy on 'The media of the past determining the politics of the future?'.

Brian always wanted to write an autobiography. He recorded loads of interviews with friends and colleagues – but never got round to it. As *It's the media, stupid!* was being completed we hit on a marvellous idea: I would interview him on Zoom about his life and ideas – and we would carry the transcript at the end of the book. I have friend and *ES* joint editor Donald Matheson to thank for alerting me to Zoom's ability to transcribe all video: so following six interviews I had enough material for a kind of 7,000-word substitute 'biography'. Brian was, above all, a conversationalist: for him, the acquisition of knowledge was a dialogic process. In a way, then, the interview at the back of the book perhaps best captures the Brian we knew and so admired.

Celebrating Brian Winston

Next in this *Ethical Space* issue, two colleagues and friends pay tribute. After Brian stepped down as chair of the Institute of Communication Ethics in 2007, he was followed by Fiona Thompson for two years – and then by John Mair in 2009. Mair, editor of more than forty texts, writes: 'Brian wrote for several of my curated book collections – on the BBC, on the pandemic and others. Always original. You gave him an idea – though usually it was the other way round – and he would run with it, put it through his institutional memory and wide reading and deliver before the deadline.' While Ivor Gaber, Brian's colleague on the editorial board of the *British Journalism Review*, highlights his 'refusal to be pigeon-holed, and his absolute commitment to factuality and the historical method'.

Florian Zollmann, a PhD student and then teacher colleague of Brian at the University of Lincoln for a number of years, reviews his last book, *The roots of fake news: Objecting to objective journalism* (Routledge, 2021) which he wrote with his son, Matthew. Zollmann concludes: 'Winston and Winston have produced a formidable study on the roots of the "fake news" crisis and how it could be mitigated. The book is a must read for scholars, students and journalists interested in understanding how the intricate relationship between journalism, truth and "fake news" has built up over centuries.'

Finally, in the tribute section, Stephen J. A Ward, in reviewing *It's the media, stupid!*, describes the essays as 'intelligent and stimulating' and adds: 'There is historical continuity amid the ten chapters: some of the main issues have been around for a long time: freedom of expression, media harm and the perennial debate on objectivity. There is also novelty: the social and media contexts in which the issues occur have changed, and the chapters reflect this evolution.' Ward also takes the opportunity to question the approaches to objectivity of a number of contributors – a challenge very much in the Winstonian tradition.

Richard Lance Keeble, editor of *It's the media, stupid!* published by Abramis, of Bury St Edmunds, ISBN: 9781845497866, £14.95. Email: publish@abramis.co.uk; phone: 01284 717884; Abramis Publishing, ASK House, Northgate Avenue, Bury St Edmunds, Suffolk IP32 6BB. The editors of *Ethical Space* would like to thank Abramis for allowing us to reproduce three of the essays from the book in this tribute edition

PAPER

Clifford G. Christians

Humans as cultural beings in theory and practice

The philosophy-of-the-human as cultural beings emphasises the intrinsic importance of our symbolic and interpretive capacities. Humans are the one living species constituted by language; therefore, humans are fundamentally cultural beings. Communication is the catalytic agent in cultural formation, and its most explicit expressions are symbolic creations such as the dramatic arts, public discourse, oral-aural language, electronic entertainment, live streaming and digital networks. Our linguistic nature means that interpretation is the key to understanding human consciousness. Interpretation takes seriously lives that are grounded in cultural complexities and, therefore, critical inquiry is interpretation's key modality. As media writer and producer, in ethics and critique, teaching and administration, Brian Winston exemplified this humanities perspective.

Keywords: critical inquiry, cultural being, interpretation, philosophy of language, symbol

The philosophy-of-the-human
The philosophy-of-the-human concerns itself with the deepest questions human beings have faced since history began. In the philosophy-of-the-human's most credible forms, the interdependence of people, animals and plant life is supposed, rather than the human species considered dominant over other animate forms. The philosophical perspective developed here privileges human mediations while committed to the unified web of organic existence.

The philosophy-of-the-human investigates the status of mortal beings in the universe and the purpose and meaning of human life. In contrast, the empirical sciences are said to be concerned with the physical, chemical and biological properties of things. The philosophical approach of this paper denies this dualism. Humans are seen as an indivisible whole, an organic unity with multi-sided sociocultural and physical capacities. The various dimensions of humanness express themselves in and through one another. Language and society are not two separate realms, with relationships that require specification; they are interactive in human livelihood. The ethnographic is embodied in human experience rather than becoming statistically abstract empiricism. Defining humans as cultural beings does not commit the fallacy of naturalistic theorising, where rationality determines both the genesis and the conclusion.

The philosophy-of-the-human presupposes that it makes sense to argue for a human reality and that philosophical scholarship is able to contribute to its comprehension. David Hume's *Treatise of human nature* (1739-1740) and Immanuel Kant's *Anthropology* (1798) took these presumptions to be uncontested. In the twentieth century, Ernst Cassirer summarised his four-volume *The philosophy of symbolic forms* (1923-1929) as an *Essay on man* and Michael Landman presents a standard label for this tradition with his title *Philosophical anthropology* (1974) (cf Ricoeur 1967; Schacht 1990). Søren Kierkegaard's *Concluding unscientific postscript: Philosophical fragments* (1941 [1846]) conceives the truth of humanity phenomenologically, as subjectivity rather than as capacities that determine actual human contingencies. For Karl Marx, in the *Sixth thesis of Feuerbach* (1845), humanity does not consist of metaphysical or in-born traits, but humans are an ensemble of social relations that are historically contingent. Jean-Paul Sartre's *Existentialism and humanism* (1973 [1946]) insists that we 'exist first and define ourselves afterwards' acquiring an essence through choices and projects, with nothing to be explained by something outside ourselves. In Friedrich Nietzsche's best-known *Human all too human: A book for free spirits* (1908 [1878]), the human analytical awareness that he called 'psychological observations' enables humans to control the narrative of their own existence. Reinhold Niebuhr's theological two-volume *The nature and destiny of man* (1943) presumes human reality also, as do *The philosophy of human nature* (2008), by Howard Kainz, and Michael Ruse's *The philosophy of human evolution* (2012) in contemporary terms. The philosophy of the human as an intellectual idea has developed a significant account of what human being entails. Without exception these works verify the philosophy-of-the-human's conceptual foundation that human reality is theoretically consequential.

Existence versus essence

As philosophers have searched for the characteristics that are both common and exclusive to human beings, one answer has focused on the epistemic category 'essence'. Essences are considered determinative of the phenomenon called humankind. To understand human nature is to grasp the necessary constituents of this bounded entity. The idea of human nature as essence is metaphysical in character, with the natural aspects of human beingness typically self-interest, humanity-interest and life-interest. The Marxist tradition is highly critical of an unalterable inner being, for example; confined to human nature, inquiry regarding essence is reductionistic. The dualisms that result from the essential approach to human nature have been dissentious and generally unproductive.

Existentialism contradicts the essentialist tradition. From Martin Heidegger's revolutionary *Being and time* (1927), the philosophy-of-the-human's prevailing emphasis has been existential Being. Heidegger's redefinition 'does not conceive of human beings in relation to a reality that transcends and constitutes them as those they are' (Schacht 1990: 161). In this new paradigm, human beingness is not an immutable essence but an animated existent expressing the meaning of things. In the existential terms of this essay, essences cannot be determinative of humankind; being-in-the-world is the primary given.

The existentialist framework views relational reality as a complex of congruent dimensions. Thus, the philosophy-of-the-human does not illuminate a static substance; rather, the reality it proposes is a multi-faceted complex of coherent dimensions. In explicating the properties of the human condition, the processes and engagements of human life are its determinants. The major concern of philosophical exploration of human existence is inter-personal relationships, that is, the ontology of communalism. Among these relationships, inter-subjectivity is the primary theme. The existential philosophical approach emphasises the cultural and historical nature of human beings, and the intrinsic importance of the symbolic and interpretive capacities, as seen in communicative action. The perspective of humans in ontological terms avoids intellectual dualisms such as formal rationality versus subjectivism.

When the philosophy-of-the-human is considered across geography and history, three properties of human existence are understood: the universal human species in cultural terms, the interpretive mode of philosophical hermeneutics, and the authentic identity of critical theory as the linguistic framework for cross-cultural theorising.

Cultural species

The philosophy-of-the-human identifies the necessary and sufficient conditions of human existence; in so doing four perspectives have dominated – biological organism, rational agent, social being and cultural species. This intellectual history is summarised here in comparative terms, with a rationale given for the preferred definition of humans as cultural beings.

Humans-as-biological-organisms is one of the foremost definitions in the philosophical literature. Humans are considered living entities within the biosphere. This understanding emphasises the continuity of human life with other animate forms, those ranging from embryonic organisms to the sophisticated systems of human agency. The biological organism scholarship includes human evolution, human evolutionary biology, population genetics, paleontology and the study of biological relatives.

In the philosophy-of-the-human tradition that considers humans to be rational beings, reasoning centres on autonomous actors. Classical Greek philosophy was committed to a basal rationalism; that is, the identity of being and reason as our essential humanness. For René Descartes (1596-1650), the essence of selfhood is thinking substance (*res cogitans*); the human species is rationality interiorised, *cogito ergo sum*. As the eighteenth century congealed around Cartesian rationality, Kant lectured in his early career on mathematics, logic and Newtonian physics at the University of Königsberg. His first major book, *Universal natural history and theory of the heavens* (1755), described the universe's structure in terms of Newton's cosmology (Kant 1781, 1785). John Stuart Mill's *Utilitarianism* (1979 [1861]) is rooted in the inductive reasoning of his *System of logic* (1843) so that an exclusive formal principle constitutes rational judgements. Based on August Comte's *A general view of positivism* (1910 [1848]), social research is neutral for Mill, ordered with statistical precision on the sophisticated procedures of inferential logic.

In the post-Enlightenment West for natural science and empirical social science, genuine knowledge is testable and, therein, objectively true. It is cognitively precise, but in linear fashion with a non-contingent starting point.

Clifford G. Christians

Truth was explained in scientific terms and rational calculation was accepted as modernity's ideology. Rationality was understood through analytic calculation that divided natural reality into quantitative items that are to be managed technically.

The definition of humans as social beings is philosophically derived from Aristotle, in the 4th century BCE. As he argues in his *Politics* (1992 [350 BCE]), human beings are social and political by nature, 'an animal intended to live in a *polis*' (ibid: 123a). Philosophers who define humans as social beings accentuate the constitutive role of social structures in human experience and action, which they find more compelling than explanations centred on the biological or rational. In this definition, as members of particular societies, human beings are 'producers as well as the products of the conditions of their existence', whose consciousness is informed by social formations and whose lives are bound up with the domain of social relations (Schacht 1990: 165). In Aristotle's tradition, the concept of essentialist human nature is presumed. Even as the tradition expands conceptually – imagination, wisdom, discernment – the notion of essence remains the intellectual core.[1]

Philosophers committed to the idea of 'social beings in the world' discuss among themselves the overriding issue whether situated existence necessitates realisation. Given the complex circumstances involved in particular situations, and contending that identity is not determined by such circumstances, what relational stances, then, does this definition entail? In Heidegger's state of fallenness, for example, wherein is resistance? Can there be distancing from social contexts without transcendence outside the situatedness? What is the alternative to illusions of false security when beingness is under assault? In what capacity is consciousness critical when insisting on cognitive neutrality?

From the perspective of humans as cultural beings, the idea of rational being is reductionist, accounting for the epistemic but not for a holistic humanity of emotions, will and *techne*. In the symbolic approach to communication, concepts are not separated from their representations. The social and personal dimensions of language are in unity.

Humans-as-biological-organisms continues to be productive, with neuroscience advancing its complexity. But the foundational concepts for the human condition remain elementary in character. Beyond the quest for survival is the need for meaningful human interaction; we comprehend ourselves by interpreting the symbolism that our lifeworld represents.

Symbolic expressions

In the philosophy-of-the-human tradition that inspires this paper, humans know themselves through their symbolic expressions. Communication is the creative process of building and affirming the human order though symbols, with cultures the human habitat that results. Language does not merely reflect reality from the outside; events must be recomposed into narratives in order for humans to comprehend reality at all. In Richard Schacht's summary definition: 'Humans are language-using and culture-incorporating creatures whose form of experience, conduct and interaction take shape in linguistically and culturally structured environments, and are conditioned by the meanings they bear' (Schacht 1990: 173).

Communication is the public agency through which human identity is realised. Language is not a vehicle of individuated cognition and subjective preference as the epistemology of rational choice assumes, but belongs to the community's reflection and action. As the alphabet organises the complex world of sound into its audiological units, humans as cultural beings use lingual formations to initiate and maintain a liveable environment.

In Ernst Cassirer's *Philosophy of symbolic forms* (1953-1957, 1966 [1923-1929]), the symbolic realm is unique to the human species. Humans alone of living entities possess the creative mind, the capacity to construct the domain of human understanding typically called 'culture'. Humanity has no essential static nature in itself, only history. History is a precondition of all thought including critical reflection. That which appears to humans in their modality of understanding is gained from history's pre-given context. Reason is not ensconced in innermost being, isolated from communication, as John Locke (1632-1704) argued; nor is reason a separate faculty. As humans create lifeworlds through language, these creations are permeated by epistemic properties such as rationale, judgement, examination and discovery.

Human beings are a cultural species, enabling them to represent different cultural identities, all of which transcend the natural behaviour of other species. To contemplate this reality philosophically is to examine such questions as: What makes cultural forms of life possible? What distinguishes culture from natural organic forms?

And what is a valid reason for acting? Moreover, the phenomenon of human intersubjectivity is philosophically interesting. Human expressions develop into further expressions and intentions are registered intermittently; together they produce other expressions that include intentionality, with all levels and dimensions conditioned by symbolic conventions.

Linguistic capacity is a structural property of cultural beingness; perception, emotion, planning and thought are all plausibly transformed into linguistic creations. Transformed connections between perception and belief are also conceivable, as are the manifold relationships between thought and action. For Michael Tomasello's *A natural history of human thinking* (2014) the lingual capacity enables joint intentionality, peculiar to humans as collaborators. Non-linguistic animals cooperate in the sense that participants in a functional task carry out their part in a social process. Collaboration goes beyond cooperation by linking the collaborators together in a form of networked minds with cognition distributed across the participants. Tomasello argues that collaborative activity creates a more permanent shared world, that is to say, a culture.

Interpretive beings
The symbolic, linguistic character of the human species means that interpretation is indispensable for understanding anthropological capacities, the vicissitudes of life and moral requisites. When humans are defined as cultural beings, human affairs are fundamentally interpretive, rather than a matter of scientific explanation presuming neutrality. Since humanity is embedded in an existing cultural world, its sense of being is necessarily historical. The world orientation of humans-in-relation is a primordial given, and no one ever stands outside an evolving interpretation of his or her humanness. It is illusory to claim a pure understanding of human reality that is non-interpretive. Because all experience is linguistic, humans understand themselves as subjects, and the world in which they live, only through the symbolic meanings that represent the world. Therefore, both philosophical analysis of and everyday observation of human affairs are matters of interpretation rather than of rational calculation.

In the philosophy-of-the-human in the West, classical Greece established the process of interpretation as ascetically radical to human life and consequently considered it an intellectual problem. Thus, Aristotle wrote a major treatise on interpretation (*hermeneia*), that is, the erudite *Peri hermeneias*, 'On Interpretation', in the *Organon*. In so delineating the conditions of understanding, Aristotle centred on the human ability to interpret languages, to make linguistic expressions meaningful. The art of *hermenia* is the key to moral judgements in the *Nicomachean ethics*. Plato had already established in the *Phaedrus* (370 BC) that messages of expression are distinct from acts of interpretation. Presuming the validity of his distinction, in the *Ion* (380 BC) Plato focuses on the role of the interpretive process within the broader category, understanding. The idea of interpretation, with varying emphases, appears in the classical literature of Lucretius, Plutarch, Euripides, Xenophon and Epicurus.

Ricoeur's theory of interpretation
The philosopher of language, Paul Ricoeur, reconstructs the philosophy of the human around the interpretive modality. Interpretation is dialogue with human existence past and present; therefore, epistemic certainty is impossible (Ricoeur 1967). No facts exist that speak for themselves. Actualities of human existence must be symbolised as interactive voices to be understood. Interpretation is a multi-dimensional activity; the materials available for interpretation are themselves interpreted: memories, beliefs, heterodoxies and perceptions, for example (cf. Gadamer 1975, 1989).

In Ricoeur's *Conflict of interpretations* (1974) and *Interpretation theory* (1976), the ontological character of his philosophy of language is developed explicitly. The awareness of humans as beings-in-the-world is based on the lingual reality of belongingness for *homo sapiens*. Human existence is a composite of present-day socioculturalism and of civilisations past that continue to exist in art, music, literature and philosophy. Self-being is always interpreted within a community of interacting beings. 'The subject that interprets himself while interpreting signs is no longer the *cogito;* rather, he is a being who discovers by the exegesis of his own life, that he is placed in Being before he places and possesses himself.' Our manner of existence 'remains from start to finish a being-interpreted' (Ricoeur 1974: 11).

Humans understand themselves as situated in time and space by interpreting the symbolic meanings that constitute the world of species existence. Subjectivity is a person's existential awareness in the ongoing interpretive process. It is invalid to assume that there is direct knowledge of our selfhood or that the self is autonomous, since conscious awareness is a construal of our cultural situatedness.

Clifford G. Christians

The idea of metaphor is the centrepiece of Ricoeur's theory of interpretation. The semantic power of metaphor engenders a surplus of meaning in the linguistic imagination. In *The rule of metaphor* (1981), he defends a new understanding of metaphor's lingual purpose. Ricoeur argues that classic rhetoric presupposed two levels of signification for metaphor – the primary literal level and the other symbolic level, which is secondary. As obvious from Ricoeur's theory of interpretation, dividing metaphor into these two domains as separate, unequal steps is erroneous. The interpretive process is fluid, with interpreters interacting between levels both erratically and simultaneously within the semiotic context. As denotation and inference indicate, words are polysemic. All languages provide metaphorical resources that can be used creatively to produce new meanings. Surplus of meaning expands and extends the original without abandoning it; there is a root idea of meaningfulness across cultures, though elaborations are multiple.

Ricoeur does not limit our understanding of discourse to its correspondence with facts or to the author's intent or to one literal meaning; he sees all forms of communication in terms of the 'principle of plentitude', that is, 'a text means all that it can mean' (Ricoeur 1981: 176). Meaning is constrained by the dialectic of context, by the history of the narrative and by the boundaries of actual experience, but the pivotal feature of interpretation is the extravagance of significations. For Ricoeur, our spatiotemporal location and transcending the local are an integrated composite. Surplus of meaning is not 'simply different meanings appended to different beliefs' (Lynch 2011: 6). Ricoeur's surplus of meaning gives multiple realisability in narrative a credible form.

Interpretation is not abstractionism; the human species cannot withdraw from its linguisticality to determine what something actually means. Interpretation is always at the level of the lingual world native to us. For Ricoeur, language is the vehicle that makes the intelligible accessible for use, with all lingual exercises interpretive. As Heidegger puts it: 'All language … interprets. It is an interpretation at one and the same time of a reality and of the one who speaks about this reality' (1971a: 89). Interpretation opens up the immanent properties of public life in its dynamic dimensions. The livelihood of humans as cultural beings is characterised by multiple interpretations and grounded in cultural diversity.

Critical inquiry
The philosophy-of-the-human as cultural being entails critical forms of knowledge production in both cognition and practice. The symbolic theory of communicative forms, and the interpretive modality that this approach requires, is the lingual arena in which critical inquiry has epistemological priority.

Critical theories share the ideas and methodologies of interpretive theories. Interpretive and critical approaches do not merely explain but establish commitments between interpreters and the interpreted. Interpretation and critical inquiry are not reportage, but both are claims of linguistic philosophy. Critical scholarship differs in that its interpretive acts are symbolic constructs to critique the ways that societies encumber and subjugate. Critical perspectives aim to change human conditions by emphasising the social structures of society as a whole.

Critical inquiry enriches interpretativeness by specialising in dialectical analysis. The art of knowing truth, by uncovering the contradictions in adversarial reasoning and in underlying commonplace ideologies, exposes the oppositional struggles for power. When people become aware of the dialectic of opposing forces, they are able to liberate themselves and change the existing order. Critical inquiry is reflective assessment that exposes power ensembles, contending as it does that a society's social degradations arise more decisively from hidden structures and cultural assumptions than from individual psychological factors.[2]

Habermas and critical inquiry
The philosophical problem that emerges in critical inquiry is identifying those aspects of its theories and methods that are adequate for underwriting social criticism. Jürgen Habermas is the principal second generation critical theorist to accomplish this task. Habermas's *Knowledge and human interests* (1968) established that critical knowledge is based on principles that differentiate it from natural science and from the liberal arts by its reflection and emancipation. Habermas's philosophical endeavour from *Knowledge and human interests* in 1968 to *Moral consciousness and communicative action* in 1990 has been to develop an interactive, fallibilist and ethnographic account of rationality, pushing critical inquiry in a naturalist direction. From the 1960s onwards, language, symbolism and meaning have been developed as the theoretical foundation of the humanities through the influence of Ludwig Wittgenstein, Ferdinand de Saussure, Hans-Georg Gadamer and

other thinkers in linguistic philosophy, symbolic interactionism and hermeneutics. Habermas's project reflects this philosophy-of-language trajectory.[3]

Already with Max Horkheimer (1895-1973) in the early days of the Frankfurt School, positivist social science was rejected for its reductionistic study of issues in isolation and its separation of facts from values through quantitative techniques. Habermas endorses the Frankfurt epistemology. For him, likewise, rationality is not the possession of knowledge. The issue is communicative rationality, that is, 'how speaking and acting subjects use knowledge' (Habermas 1984: 11). In this view, speech acts ought to reconstruct an equalitarian domain in which participants are 'attributed the capacity to produce valid utterances and are considered capable of distinguishing valid from invalid expressions' (Habermas 1990: 31). Acquiring the abilities needed for communicative rationality enables critical inquiry.

Thus, Habermas redefines critical inquiry as reconstructive science. Habermas's reconstructionism explicates the conditions for incorrect or correct utterances; reconstruction also explains why some utterances distort, some speech acts are unsuccessful and argumentation frequently inadequate. Habermas uses formal pragmatics philosophically to identify the justifications used in various forms of argumentation; these reflections yield semantic rules that organise discursive communication which, in turn, can reform discursive institutions (Habermas 1996: 230n). Reconstructive theory and practice 'explain deviant cases and through this indirect authority acquire a critical function' (Habermas 1990: 32). As noted regarding ideological speech, Habermas calls narrative that is not dependent on the conditions of communicative rationality distorted communication. In such communication, interactants are not able to participate fairly regardless of the outcome.

Ideology of instrumentalism

Ideology is the central concept in the scholarship of critical inquiry, that is, ideology as ideas that configure societies' notion of reality. In critical inquiry, ideology as a system of representations that governs how social orders are constructed is the principal obstacle to human liberation. Although Habermas quarrelled with marginal issues in Adorno and Horkheimer's *Dialectic of enlightenment* (2003 [1944]), he reiterated their historical treatment that modernity's reason and freedom have turned into their opposites; rather than liberating, the Western Enlightenment's worldview – that the mind deliberates impartially – has become a dominating and controlling ideology.[4]

The prevailing ideology in the industrial West is instrumentalism – the idea that technology is neutral and expands in terms of its own technical character without conditioning our humanness. Technologies are considered artifacts of science apart from values. Technological products are thought to be independent, being used to support both positive and negative lifestyles and cultures. 'Technology, as pure instrumentality, is indifferent to the variety of ends it can be employed to achieve' (Feenberg 1991: 5). Websites provide both the lives of heroes and the rancorous hate speech of fundamentalist sects. As ideology, the idea of instrumental neutrality is taken for granted.

In instrumentalism, or its cognate technicism, as digital technologies represent reality they do so with a technological rhythm. Human values are replaced by efficiency, that is, by the machine's defining feature. This is a mechanical model where the capabilities of media technologies set a society's agenda and establish the cultural issues. With its diffusion-of-tools mentality, instrumentalism begins and ends with the technological reality itself and offers strategies for accomplishing technical goals through it. In the ideology of instrumentalism, scientific prowess and financial resources are channelled into high technology, into improving the power and speed of technological instruments. Humans participate in cyberspace as the facilitators of networks. Critical inquiry, in exposing the ideology of neutral instruments, examines symbolic systems in their historical and institutional contexts – instead of a preoccupation with subsets of hardware and software.[5]

Monopoly of knowledge

The Canadian communications theorist, Harold Innis, has expanded critical inquiry with his concept 'monopoly of knowledge'. Critical inquiry has included a psychological orientation since Erich Fromm's *Escape from freedom* (1941) and Innis's *The bias of communication* (1951) benefits from that intellectual trajectory. But his major influence on critical perspectives is sociological, clarifying in *Empire and communication* (1952) the compositional and historical dimensions of media ecology. For Innis, media technologies do not exist innocuously alongside one another. As his historical studies elaborated, new technologies of communication tend to monopolise human knowledge and reduce existing media forms to a supplementary role.

Clifford G. Christians

From the introduction of cuneiform writing to contemporary communication satellites, fibre optics and the algorithmic digital, scholars in the Innis tradition examine all important shifts in symbolic forms, associating them with differentiations in culture and in social organisation. The conceptual demand is to identify the distinctive properties of particular media technologies such as books, magazines, radio, cinema, television, live stream, Facebook, WhatsApp, Twitter, YouNow and WeChat. As Innis concludes, oral culture continued after print became the dominant medium, but the oral-aural mode was no longer the standard of truth or the centrepiece of medicine, engineering, law and politics. In the era of ideological instrumentalism, digital knowledge is primary and other print and broadcast forms become secondary. Cyberspace monopolises our livelihood and institutions now.

A credible critical approach in the internet age must account for this monopoly-of-knowledge phenomenon. Learning from the Innis tradition, the imperative for critical inquiry in the ideological era of instrumentalism is multimedia abundance instead of the Web 2.0's monopoly of knowledge.

Perspectivism
Perspective-taking is implicit in the reflexivity of critical inquiry. Since the critical approach focuses on social relationships, such relationships can be specified in terms of perspective-takers by those who are included in the interpretations. Habermas calls the social inquiries 'technocratic' that use methodologies for problem-solving in terms of third-person knowledge of impersonal consequences. For critical inquiry, reflective participants are contextualised in the social relationships they constitute, enabling them to discern across various perspectives in their acts of social criticism. When there is multimedia abundance, it is possible to replace the social scientist as detached observer with a diversity of critical perspectives.

Critical perspectives disclose; they open up the inside meaning to critique the heart of the matter. Critical perspectives see beneath the surface of everyday affairs, taking account of the interactional context, motives and presuppositions. Thus, authentic disclosure is opposed to the ideology of instrumentalism. These inside perspectives that reveal the inner meaning of the lingual world in which humans exist are presented in the natural languages of human interaction. Natural language rather than the artificial languages of mathematical statistics or linear induction is the mode of perspectivism.

Critical perspectives in narrative form are a society's critical discourse and mediated technologies are the principal public forum of critical discourse.[6] Given humans as cultural beings and technologies as processes of cultural formation, communication technology is not a tool *per se*, but a cultural process of making meaning. From the perspective of technology as a cultural enterprise, media technologies symbolise human events without which the human species cannot exist. Thus, communicative events such as educational pedagogy, medical networks and entertainment programming are not driven by context-free abstractions, but resonate with the breadth of human agency in its interactions with animate and inanimate reality. The existence of culture presupposes the reflexive ability of the human mind to interpret culture and its contexts. The interpretive turn recovers history and biography, so that complex perspective-taking and multi-layered events and cultures are represented adequately, with critical discourse the result.

Symbolic systems
As contended above, the philosophy-of-humans as the cultural species considers the lingual arts as the defining characteristic of human existence, language referring in expansive terms to the full range of symbolic forms. Stated differently, communication is the catalytic agent in cultural formation and its most explicit expressions are symbolic formations: the dramatic arts, news narrative, oral-aural language, electronic entertainment, live streaming and digital networks. Since language is the material of human exchange, symbols create what humans view as reality. The primary constituents of human livelihood are religion, myth, art, science and history; symbols are the facilitator of all such creations. Symbols are not identical to the actualities they symbolise, but they do participate in the authentication of that which they represent. In literature and cinema or YouTube Live, as examples of symbolic formations, their inner dialectics – point of departure, setting, tone, digital coding and resolution of conflict – reflect their culture's value system.

Symbolic systems of critical discourse in the public forum will follow the interpretive arts to sufficiency. Mediations that inform the public adequately aim for interpretive adequacy. Interpretation with a critical perspective is not preoccupied with specific struggles, but addresses the dominant and resilient crises of having social science, education, neighbourhoods, religious centres and voluntary associations co-opted by the ideology of technicism. What

Clifford Geertz (1973) calls 'thick description' replaces the thinness of statistically precise objectivism. Accounts that meet the principle of sufficiency put specifics in their context of meaning. Sufficiency entails credible interpretations of the attitudes, language and cultural forms of the social group being reported. News as critical discourse means distinguishing the major components of the lifeworld being investigated from digressions and parentheses. Interpretive adequacy in the public arena challenges the injustices of hegemonic alliances and supports movements opposing these disenfranchisements, recognising the activists as reflective participants in cultural formation.

Critical inquiry appeals to the knowledge that reflective agents already possess to a greater or lesser extent. Critical social scientists participate in the creation of the contexts in which their perspective-taking is publicly verified. The emphasis in interpretation is on discovery rather than administering routinised procedures. According to Habermas's communicative rationality, the goal of critical inquiry is not to manipulate or control sociocultural processes, but to initiate and foster critical discourse so that there is adequate participatory reflection by all those affected (Habermas 1971: 40-41).

Conclusion

For the philosophy-of-the-human, the issue is not the certainty of knowledge but theory as inquiry into the meaning of metanarratives. Theorising discloses the fundamental conditions of existential reality. The suggestiveness of theoretical claims derives from the interpretive domain that is symbolised in human culture. Theories are not scholastic paradigms of mathematical precision, but theorising is the imaginative power that gives an inside perspective on reality.[7] Critical theory, as in Habermas, is based on the philosophy of cultural beings as its existential ground. Thus, its orientating basis affirms the need for a strong claim of rightness in critical discourse, without which it would be invalid to engage in social criticism.

As the intellectual history of the philosophy-of-the-human documents, the question of theory is finally ontological, that is, theory concerns the nature of organic being, specifically the character of human beingness. Following Heidegger and Ellul, as argued in Innis's theory of communication, and presumed in Habermas's communicative rationality, technologies and beingness are interwoven. Therefore, mechanistic and bureaucratic standards for judging communication phenomena are decidedly secondary to cultural humanity as a normative ideal. Reality is not to be understood as a raw aggregate of the inanimate, but a converged order of material and organic that makes critical theory intelligible.[8] Knowledge is incoherent if infinite regression is presumed. Interpretation is impossible without a given. Theories are perspectival schemes for elaborating basic values.

As interpretive formulae, theories are validated by the extent to which they open up possibilities of action. Theories are not epistemically independent, but forms of discovery that are tested by the criterion of interpretive adequacy. The ethnographic is grafted into human existence rather than isolating itself as regression vectors, syllogisms and statistical correlations. The philosophy of humans as cultural beings defines agency within the ideology of instrumentalism. This philosophy-of-the-human perspective avoids the logical mistake of interpreting cultural diversity as moral relativism. It recognises that asserting prescriptive claims from the experiential commits the fallacy of confused categories.

Brian Winston, as media writer and documentary film producer, in ethics and critique, teaching and administration, exemplified the humanities perspective of this essay. As a world class critical theorist, his hermeneutical depth on mediated symbolic systems demonstrates how interpretive scholarship ought to be done in a global era of cross-cultural complexity.

Notes

[1] Marx's existentialism is an alternative to Aristotelian essence, contending that the social organism is greater than the sum of its parts. According to this organicist model originating with Hegel, what is real to the social organism's members can only be real in relation to the whole. Society is not a conglomerate of atomistic individuals as in Locke's contractual notion of society

[2] The history and content of critical theory is well known and, therefore, acknowledged in this footnote rather than elaborated in the text. The Frankfurt School of Critical Theory is the most influential tradition, founded in 1923 at the Institute of Social Research of the University of Frankfurt. Max Horkheimer was director from 1930 to 1958 stressing interdisciplinary scholarship, with Theodor Adorno (philosopher and sociologist) and Erich Fromm (psychologist) early collaborators, and literary critics, Walter Benjamin and Leo Lowenthal, later associates. The institute disbanded in 1969 but its transformations continued in new and extensive form with Jürgen Habermas. Habermas's communicative rationality, politics of textuality and dialectical discourse are particularly relevant to the philosophy of humans as cultural beings

[3] Social philosopher Max Weber is also influential for Habermas. Weber's critical perspective resulted from his recognising social science as causal and interpretive and uniting both dimensions in such publications as his *Protestant ethic and the spirit of capitalism* (1904-1905), multiple chapters in *The methodology of the social sciences* (1949) and his essay 'Science as a vocation' In his *From Max Weber: Essays in sociology* (1916)

Clifford G. Christians

[4] René Descartes's *Discourse on method* (2021 [1637]) establishes and elaborates on this objectivism, with pure mathematics the least touched by circumstances (see also Descartes 1964). For the Enlightenment mind, Descartes defines out of existence the brilliant thinking of earlier cultures and non-Western peoples

[5] In the scholarship of French philosopher, Jacques Ellul, modern means of communication are not neutral instruments. Media systems are absorbed into an efficiency-dominated culture. In his *Propaganda, humiliation of the word* (1965) and *The technological bluff* (1990), Ellul defines the electronic media in terms of *la technique*. This concept is for him an internal bureaucratising that saturates culture and institutions. Humans are absorbed into a data world of one-dimensional shibboleths and memes. News and entertainment media provide a rationale for human existence, with communication technologies the public perimeter of the technological order

[6] The Frankfurt School considers the mass media an oppressive technological system. Habermasian critical inquiry uses a broader definition of the mass media as a 'consciousness-shaping institution'

[7] In Thomas Kuhn's classic *The structure of scientific revolutions* (1996), theories as paradigm constructions are a complex of politics, creativity, intuition and beliefs. For Kuhn, as with this paper, theories are constructed paradigms rather than the normal science of verifying hypotheses

[8] Zygmunt Bauman's (2005) liquid modernity as an intellectual framework is also consistent with the philosophy of cultural beings. In Bauman's *Liquid life*, cultural systems and social structures have become fluid. In Grant Kien's *Global technography: Ethnography in the age of mobility* (2009), there has been a paradigmatic transformation to instability in the social media era. He follows Heidegger's *On the way to language* (1971a) and his *Poetry, language, thought* (1971b) in arguing that humans require the structure of time and a sense of distance to avoid solipsism. However, with the compression of history into the momentary and the demise of spatial limits, our basis of knowing shifts to an anywhere, anytime experience with humans seeing themselves as existing everywhere always and nowhere never

References

Aristotle (1992 [350 BCE]) *The politics*, trans. Sinclair, T. A., London, Penguin Books

Aristotle (1998 [340 BCE]) *The Nicomachean ethics*, trans. Ross, W. D., New York, Oxford University Press

Bauman, Zygmunt (2005) *Liquid life*, Cambridge, UK, Polity Press

Cassirer, Ernst (1944) *An essay on man: An introduction to a philosophy of human culture*, New Haven, CT, Yale University Press

Cassirer, Ernst (1953-1957, 1966 [1923-1929]) *The philosophy of symbolic forms*, trans. Manheim, R. and Krois, J. 4 Vols, New Haven, CT, Yale University Press

Comte, Auguste (1910 [1848]) *A general view of positivism*, trans. Bridges, J. H., London, George Routledge & Sons

Descartes, René (1964) *Rules for the direction of the mind: Philosophical essays*, trans. Lafleur, L. J., Indianapolis, Bobbs-Merrill pp 147-236. Original work began in 1628 but not published in his lifetime

Descartes, René (2021 [1637]) *Discourse on method*, trans. Veitch, J., Ottawa, East India Publishing Company

Ellul, Jacques (1954) *The technological society*, trans. Wilkinson, J., New York, Random Vintage

Ellul, Jacques (1965) *Propaganda: The formation of men's attitudes*, trans. Kellen, K. and Lerner, J., New York, Alfred A. Knopf

Ellul, Jacques (1985) *The humiliation of the word*, trans. Hanks, J. M., Grand Rapids, MI, Eerdmans

Ellul, Jacques (1990) *The technological bluff*, trans. Bromiley, G. W., Grand Rapids, MI, Eerdmans

Feenberg, Andrew (1991) *A critical theory of technology*, New York, Oxford University Press

Fromm, Erich (1941) *Escape from freedom*, New York, Henry Holt & Co

Gadamer, Hans-Georg (1975) The problem of historical consciousness, *Graduate Faculty Philosophy Journal*, New School for Social Research, Vol. 5, No. 1 pp 8-52

Gadamer, Hans-Georg (1989) *Truth and method*, trans. Weinsheimer, J. and Marshall, D. G., London, Continuum, revised edition

Geertz, Clifford (1973) *The interpretation of cultures*, New York, Basic Books

Habermas, Jürgen (1968) *Knowledge and human interests*, Boston, Beacon Press

Habermas, Jürgen (1987 [1984]) *The theory of communicative action, Vols 1 and 2*, Boston, Beacon Press

Habermas, Jürgen (1990) *Moral consciousness and communicative action*, Cambridge, MA, MIT Press

Habermas, Jürgen (1996) *Between facts and norms*, Cambridge, MA, MIT Press

Heidegger, Martin (1962 [1927]) *Being and time*, trans. Macquarrie, J. and Robinson, E., New York, Harper & Row

Heidegger, Martin (1971a) *On the way to language*, trans. Hertz, P. and Stambaugh, J., New York, Harper & Row

Heidegger, Martin (1971b) *Poetry, language, thought*, trans. Hofstader, A., New York, Harper & Row

Heidegger, Martin (1977) *The question concerning technology and other essays*, trans. Lovitt, W., New York, Harper & Row

Horkheimer, Max and Adorno, Theodor W. (2003 [1944]) *Dialectic of enlightenment*, trans. Jephcott, E., Stanford, CA, Stanford University Press

Innis, Harold (1951) *The bias of communication*, Toronto, University of Toronto Press

Innis, Harold (1952) *Empire and communication*, Toronto, University of Toronto Press

Kainz, Howard P. (2008) *The philosophy of human nature*, Chicago, Open Court Publishing

Kant, Immanuel (2016 [1781]) *Critique of pure reason*, trans. Meiklejohn, J., Auckland, Pantianos Classics

Kant, Immanuel (2009 [1785]) *Groundwork of the metaphysic of morals*, trans. Paton, H. J., New York, Harper Perennial

Kien, Grant (2009) *Global technography: Ethnography in an age of mobility*, New York, Peter Lang

Kierkegaard, Søren (1941 [1846]) *Concluding unscientific postscript: Philosophical fragments*, Princeton, NJ, Princeton University Press

Kuhn, Thomas S. (1996) *The structure of scientific revolutions*, Chicago, University of Chicago Press, third edition

Landman, Michael (1974) *Philosophical anthropology*, trans. Parent, D. J., Philadelphia, Westminster Press

Lynch, Jake (2011) *Truth as one and many*, New York, Oxford Clarendon

Mill, John Stuart (1888 [1843]) *A system of logic, ratiocinative and inductive*, New York, Harper & Brothers, eighth edition

Mill, John Stuart (1979 [1861]) *Utilitarianism*, Indianapolis, Hackett

Niebuhr, Reinhold (1964 [1941]) *The nature and destiny of man, Vol. 1: Human Nature, Vol. 2: Human destiny*, New York, Scribner's

Nietzsche, Friedrich (1908 [1878]) *Human all too human: A book for free spirits*, trans. Harvey, A., Chicago, Charles H. Kerr & Company

Ricoeur, Paul (1967) The antinomy of human reality and the problem of philosophical anthropology, Lawrence, N. and O'Connor, D. (eds) *Readings in existential phenomenology*, Englewood Cliffs, N. J., Prentice-Hall pp 390-402

Ricoeur, Paul (1974) *The conflict of interpretations: Essays in hermeneutics*, Ihde, D. (ed.) Evanston, Ill., Northwestern University Press

Ricoeur, Paul (1976) *Interpretation theory: Discourse and the surplus of meaning,* Fort Worth, Texas Christian University Press

Ricoeur, Paul (1981) *The rule of metaphor: The creation of meaning in language,* London, Routledge

Ruse, Michael (2012) *The philosophy of human evolution,* Cambridge, UK, Cambridge University Press

Sartre, Jean-Paul (1973 [1946]) *Existentialism and humanism,* trans. Mairet, P., London, Methuen

Schacht, Richard (1974) On existentialism, *existenz*-philosophy, and philosophical anthropology, *American Philosophical Quarterly,* Vol. 11, No. 4 pp 291-305

Schacht, Richard (1990) Philosophical anthropology: What, why and how, *Philosophy and Phenomenological Research,* Vol. 50 (Supplement) pp 155-176

Tomasello, Michael (2014) *A natural history of human thinking,* Cambridge, MA., Harvard University Press

Weber, Max (1992 [1904-1905]) *The Protestant ethic and the spirit of capitalism,* trans. Parsons, T., London, Routledge

Weber, Max (1946 [1919]) *From Max Weber: Essays in sociology,* Gerth, H. H. and Wright Mills, C. (eds) Oxford, Oxford University Press

Weber, Max (1949) *The methodology of the social sciences,* Shils, E. A. and Finch, H. A. (eds) New York, The Free Press

Note on the contributor

Clifford G. Christians (PhD, LittD, DHL) is Research Professor of Communications, Professor of Journalism and Professor of Media Studies Emeritus at the University of Illinois USA, where he was Director of the Institute of Communications Research and Head of the PhD in Communications for 16 years. His recent publications as author or co-author include *Key concepts in critical cultural studies, Ethics for public communication, Normative theories of the media, Media ethics: Cases and moral reasoning* (11th edition) and *Media ethics and global justice in the digital age.*

PAPER

Julian Petley

How the UK government threatens to impose online censorship

In this paper, I examine Brian Winston's defence of freedom of expression as a key Enlightenment principle and his criticisms of broadcasting regulation in the UK for departing from it. I also focus on the notion of harm, deriving from John Stuart Mill, that Winston employs to indicate where the limits of freedom of expression should lie. Winston complains that notions of offence and insult have increasingly expanded definitions of harm and so narrowed the bounds of freedom of expression. I use this critique as the starting point for an analysis of the regime of online regulation currently being proposed by the UK government in the form of the Online Safety Bill. This, I argue, threatens to create an unwieldy, unaccountable and unnecessary state apparatus of online censorship, operates with far too broad and vague a notion of harm, and will see material expelled from the online world which is entirely legal in the offline world. I conclude by examining recent proposals from the Law Commission for bringing the regulation of certain categories of online and offline communications into line, and for clarifying what is actually meant by harm in certain specific pieces of legislation. I argue that the commission's carefully delimited approach to the issue of harm in the communications sphere is greatly preferable to the regulatory Behemoth proposed by the Online Safety Bill, which would very seriously endanger the communicative freedoms espoused by Brian Winston.

Keywords: harm, offence, freedom of expression, Online Safety Bill, Ofcom

On failing to obtain freedom of expression

Brian Winston was always a redoubtable defender of freedom of expression, both as a television practitioner and as an academic, and a severe critic of those who deny or backslide on this key Enlightenment principle. Quoting Tom Paine's observation that 'what we obtain too cheap, we esteem too lightly', he lamented in *Messages: Free expression, media and the West from Gutenberg to Google* that:

> For the West, there is little or no sense that we have 'obtained' free expression and the rest of the Enlightenment's cluster of fundamental rights cheaply, or indeed at any price at all. They are simply 'there' and, 50 years after the defeat of totalitarianism in the West and some years since its fall in Eastern Europe, the struggles that secured those releases are sufficiently forgotten for these rights to be subjected to fundamental criticism and dismissal. It becomes respectable for repressive opinion once more to question their very validity as concepts; or, at best, to demand that 'responsibilities', beyond those required in general by civil society, 'pay' in some way for such rights (2005: 396).

In Winston's view, the media today enjoy less freedom than did the press in the nineteenth century, 'partial and inadequate' though this was in practice: 'Beyond its extension from person to press, the universality of free expression was not established. It remains not established today' (ibid.: 397). Such an argument would appear to fly in the face of those who still argue, like latter-day Mary Whitehouses, that the modern media are far too 'permissive', as Winston himself admits:

> In a world awash with pornography, telephoto lenses and audio bugging devices, where indeed anything seems to go, there would seem to be no basis for concern for media liberty; yet behind this flood the basics of free expression, as a concept receiving widespread support, are being eroded (ibid: 399).

Thus, while there has undoubtedly been a superficial liberalisation of the rules governing entertainment on the numerous screens which increasingly dominate our lives, at the same time the laws relating to official secrecy, terrorism, academic practice and the right to protest, for example, are being relentlessly tightened in a manner that severely limits freedom of expression in matters which are vital to the health of a democratic society (Article 19 2020). Yet, particularly in the UK, these fail to excite critical comment in much of the mainstream media. Indeed, in the case of sections of the Conservative press, such measures are all too frequently advocated and welcomed.

'An appropriate level of freedom of expression'
Nor is it the case, as is all too often supposed, that, because of the nature of the technology involved, newer media are less easy to regulate than their predecessors. To illustrate this point, Winston takes the case of television as regulated by the Communications Act 2003. This created the Office of Communications (Ofcom) and laid down that one of its duties was 'the application, in the case of all television and radio services, of standards that provide adequate protection to members of the public from the inclusion of offensive and harmful material in such services' and that it carried out this function 'in the manner that best guarantees an *appropriate* level of freedom of expression' (emphasis added). Winston's objection to Ofcom is that the regulation of the media for which it is responsible is:

> … determined by statutory bureaucratic structures beyond the courts. Such a situation would not be acceptable if applied to the press or stage, but a slough of reasons is usually given to justify why, in a liberal society, supposedly committed to free expression, differences of treatment between media can be justified (2005: 397).

Chief amongst these are the allegedly harmful 'effects' of the electronic media:

> The influence of non-print mass-communication systems is deemed so vast that they cannot be allowed to function without special extra control. Yet, it is not an absolute given that, for example, the newer media are more 'influential', for all that they are certainly more pervasive (ibid: 397-398).

In Winston's view, however, 'free expression should not be abridged by assumptions about the supposed "power" and pervasiveness of different media. Technology should have nothing to do with it as a principle'. Instead, 'the media – new, old and to come – like all individual citizens, should stand equal before the law' (ibid: 399).

Toleration's limits
In *The Rushdie fatwa and after: A lesson to the circumspect*, Winston returns to the notion of harm as a common justification for censorship. He begins by stating that 'toleration is the foundation of a right of free expression; without the one there cannot be the other' (2014: 8), before going on to note that 'toleration's limit is most clearly reached when any sort of demonstrable damage can be proved, whatever its cause' (ibid: 10). Here, Winston is drawing on J. S. Mill's famous dictum that 'the only purpose for which power can be rightfully exercised over any member of a civilised community, against his will, is to prevent harm to others' (1985 [1859]: 68). Mill also describes harmful actions as those which are 'calculated to produce evil to someone else' (ibid) or which are 'hurtful to others' (ibid: 70). Winston argues that 'harm' here equates to 'perceptible hurt' and that as 'remedies exist at law for the perceptible hurts arising from violence', so they should for speech if:

> … damage flows from it and is externally verifiable, 'perceptible'. There is a difference between the impact of a word and that of a closed fist, but words do impact none the less and their damage can be perceptible. Therefore they can be censored (Winston 2014: 11).

As an example of a law designed to deal with such damage, Winston cites the Defamation Act 2013. This lays down that a statement is defamatory if it has caused, or is likely to cause, serious harm to the claimant's reputation – a factual proposition which can be established only by referring to the actual impact of the words used. For example, a company claiming that it had been defamed would have to show that the material in question had caused it, or was likely to cause it, serious financial loss. One might also point to the Suicide Act 1961, which makes it an offence to encourage or assist suicide.

'A right not to be offended or insulted'
However, for Winston the problem is that, in practice, matters have been moving away from considering speech to be damaging only if its deleterious impact is externally verifiable and that:

> … now the 'hurts' arising from speech are not necessarily at all perceptible and indeed do not have to be present. That they could occur is enough. … Expression's potential for causing damage without specific actual damage being demonstrated is enough (ibid: 11).

Winston was particularly concerned about the Rushdie affair because, for him, it demonstrated that the principle of 'do no harm' had expanded 'to encompass a right not to be offended or insulted' (ibid: 17). It is important to understand here that he was not denying that words may, indeed, insult and offend, but, rather, arguing that these are 'effects which cannot be determined by the measure of externally verifiable damage. ... Feelings, in the nature of the case, must be self-attested; they cannot be unambiguously externally verified as can the effects of "violence"' (ibid). In Winston's view, expanding the notion of harm into what he calls this 'evidence-free, ill-defined terrain' is to give the censor:

> ... entrance to the country of offence unless the damage is perceptible (that is, externally evidenced) or perceptible damage is probable. (The law knows how to deal with probabilities). Simply to state that words can be (and do) evil in no way addresses how to deal with them in a free society (ibid: 87).

The Online Harms White Paper
However, the principles enunciated by Winston threaten to be effectively trampled underfoot by the manner in which the present British government proposes to censor the internet, which also provides ample confirmation of Winston's contention at the start of this paper that 'there is little or no sense that we have "obtained" free expression' and that 'the influence of non-print mass-communication systems is deemed so vast that they cannot be allowed to function without special extra control'.

Successive British governments have threatened to impose internet censorship ever since the World Wide Web began to enter everyday use in 1993-1994, and although various piecemeal forms of censorship have been introduced since then, nothing as totalising and all-embracing as the system outlined in the Online Harms White Paper in April 2019 has been attempted in the UK – or, indeed, in any other democratic country. As the White Paper itself put it:

- There is currently a patchwork of regulation and voluntary initiatives aimed at addressing these problems, but these have not gone far or fast enough to keep UK users safe online.

- The UK will be the first to tackle online harms in a coherent, single regulatory framework that reflects our commitment to a free, open and secure internet (Department for Digital, Culture, Media and Sport/Home Office 2019: 30).

Just how the degree of censorship outlined below can also be squared with a commitment to freedom and openness is not explained. But it is clear from the White Paper that the government intends to legislate for a statutory 'duty of care' on social media platforms and a wide range of other internet companies that 'allow users to share or discover user-generated content, or interact with each other online' (ibid: 8). This duty would require them to 'take more responsibility for the safety of their users and tackle harm caused by content or activity on their services' (ibid: 7). Crucially, it would apply not only to illegal content but also to lawful material regarded as harmful under the new legislation. The duty would be overseen by a regulator (later designated as Ofcom) armed with the power to fine companies for non-compliance. Again, anything further away from Winston's contentions that all media should stand equal before the law, and that only illegal material should be subject to censorship, is extremely hard to imagine.

The White Paper provides a list of specific harms that would be in scope of the new legislation. However, it also notes that the list is neither exhaustive nor fixed, 'as a static list could prevent swift regulatory action to address new forms of online harm, new technologies, content and new online activities' (ibid: 30). Thus, the regulator will be able to add new harms at will. The harms with which the White Paper is concerned are of three kinds: 'harms with a clear definition', 'harms with a less clear definition' and 'underage exposure to legal content' (ibid: 31). The first category is concerned with content that is already illegal under existing laws, and consists of:

- child sexual exploitation and abuse;
- terrorist content and activity;
- organised immigration crime;
- modern slavery;
- extreme pornography;
- revenge pornography;
- harassment and cyberstalking;
- hate crime;
- encouraging or assisting suicide;
- incitement of violence;
- sale of illegal goods/services, such as drugs and weapons (on the open internet);
- content illegally uploaded from prisons;
- sexting of indecent images by under-18s (creating, possessing, copying or distributing indecent or sexual images of children and young people under the age of 18).

'Harms with a less clear definition' are:

- cyberbullying and trolling;
- extremist content and activity;
- coercive behaviour;
- intimidation;
- disinformation;
- violent content;
- advocacy of self-harm;
- promotion of Female Genital Mutilation (FGM);

Finally, 'underage exposure to legal content' is defined as:

- children accessing pornography;
- children accessing inappropriate material (including under-13s using social media and under-18s using dating apps; excessive screen time).

Clearly, the second category of harms brings within the scope of the proposed legislation a whole host of material which is currently legal but is nonetheless to be banished from vast swathes of the internet, as far as its UK users are concerned, because it is considered harmful.

'An amorphous concept'

The Online Harms White Paper and the subsequent Online Safety Bill raise with glaring clarity all the problems associated with allegedly harmful media content noted repeatedly by Brian Winston. Indeed, one of the most authoritative critics of this measure, the lawyer Graham Smith (2019), echoed Winston in a blog post just after the publication of the White Paper:

> Harm is an amorphous concept. It changes shape according to the opinion of whoever is empowered to apply it. Even when limited to harm suffered by an individual, harm is an ambiguous term. It will certainly include objectively ascertainable physical injury. ... But it may include also include subjective harms, dependent on someone's opinion that they have suffered what they regard as harm. When applied to speech, this is highly problematic. ... Harm as such has no identifiable boundaries, at least none that would pass a legislative test.

Just how broadly the government wished at this point to define harm can be illustrated by the inclusion in the White Paper of 'threats to our way of life'. This is defined in a highly Panglossian manner with which many would strongly disagree ('our society is built on confidence in public institutions, trust in electoral processes, a robust, lively and plural media, and hard-won democratic freedoms that allow different voices, views and opinions to freely and peacefully contribute to public discourse'). The main harm to this idealised vision is seen as stemming from inaccurate information and disinformation, the latter defined here as 'information which is created or disseminated with the deliberate intent to mislead; this could be to cause harm, or for personal, political or financial gain' and material which 'can threaten public safety, undermine national security, fracture community cohesion and reduce trust' (2019: 22). In which case, the legally proper solution would be to frame legislation making it a specific offence to spread inaccurate information and disinformation in any form of media whatsoever – a measure which, of course, would never be introduced as it would cause apoplexy amongst the government's many supporters in the national press. Thus, the government finds it more convenient to stigmatise the internet while banging the patriotic drum and, as Smith (2019) puts it, to engage in the kind of prose that 'may benefit the soapbox or an election manifesto but has no place in or near legislation'.

Similar points about the need for specific legislation to tackle specific harms were made by, amongst many others, Index on Censorship and the Open Rights Group. The former argued that:

> The wide range of different harms which the government is seeking to tackle in this policy process require different, tailored responses. Measures proposed must be underpinned by strong evidence, both of the likely scale of the harm and the measures' likely effectiveness. ... Any legislative or regulatory measures should be supported by clear and unambiguous evidence of their need and effectiveness (2019).

Likewise, the Open Rights Group stated:

> Any policy intervention must be underpinned with a clear, objective evidence base which demonstrates that actions are necessary and proportionate. Regulation impacting on citizens' free speech needs to be based on evidence of harm traceable to specific pieces or types of content, activity or behaviour, rather than expectations or social judgements that these may be related to possible harms. ... Any policy intervention must be defined and limited by precise terminology. Imprecise language risks dangerous overreach. If the harms-based model of regulation is used, tighter identification/definition of types of harms and their natures is vitally needed (2019: 4-5).

Julian Petley

The draft Online Safety Bill

In its full response in December 2020 to the consultation process initiated by the White Paper, the government narrowed its definition of harmful online content and activity to material which 'gives rise to a foreseeable risk of significant adverse physical or psychological impact on individuals' (Department for Digital, Culture, Media and Sport/Home Office 2020: 24). It also made it clear that 'the duty of care will apply to content or activity which could cause significant physical or psychological harm to an individual' (ibid: 50). The proposed measure was now more focused on personal safety as properly understood rather than vague and unbounded notions of harm – which is presumably why it was renamed the Online Safety Bill. However, as Smith (2020) points out:

> The definition of harm remains problematic: not least because inclusion of 'psychological impact' may suggest that the notion of harm is still tied to variable, subjective reactions of different readers. Subjectivity opens the door to application of a standard of the most easily upset user.

The draft Online Safety Bill was published in May 2021. According to its impact assessment, it seeks to address the following broad categories of harmful online content:

- Illegal user-generated content and activity: user-generated content and activity which is an offence under UK law – such as child sexual exploitation and abuse, terrorism, hate crime and sale of illegal drugs and weapons.
- Legal but harmful user-generated content and activity: user-generated content and activity which may not be illegal under all circumstances, but which gives rise to a foreseeable risk of psychological and physical harm to adults – such as abuse or eating disorder content.
- Underage exposure to user-generated content and activity which gives rise to a foreseeable risk of psychological and physical harm to children – such as pornography, violent content (Department for Digital, Culture, Media and Sport/Home Office 2021: 20).

It also refers back to the White Paper's list of harms of various kinds, which shows that these are still very much in play. Furthermore, the problematic phrase 'legal but harmful' occurs no less than 97 times, although the document is worryingly short on specific examples of such material, other than 'abuse, harassment and intimidation directed towards public figures' and 'cyberbullying'. Harm is defined in the draft Bill at section 137(1) as simply 'physical or psychological harm', which is a shortened version of the definition proposed by the government in its full response. However, as Smith (2021) notes:

> The draft Bill does not stipulate that 'harmful' should be understood in the same limited way. The result of that omission, combined with other definitions, could be to give the Secretary of State regulation-making powers for legal but harmful content that are, on the face of them, not limited to physical or psychological harm.

On the other hand, in the case of legal but harmful content it does provide a more developed version of the full response's general definition of harm by specifying that the impact of allegedly harmful material must be on a hypothetical adult or child 'of ordinary sensibilities', that is, not the most easily upset user.

'Working out what harm means'

The government finally published the Online Safety Bill on 17 March 2022, after the final draft of this article was written. Unsurprisingly, its conception of harm bears little or no relation to the one advanced by Brian Winston, takes no account of his (and others') argument that specific harms should be the subject of specific laws and turns on its head his contention that all media should be treated equally before the law. Indeed, all of these ideas are summarily dismissed in the report by Lorna Woods and William Perrin for the Carnegie UK Trust, *Online harm reduction? A statutory duty of care and regulator*, which was published concurrently with the White Paper and greatly informed government thinking on this matter. They state:

> A traditional focus for the debate on internet harms has been the 'if it is illegal offline it should be illegal online' and then to focus on the removal of content that is contrary to the criminal law. While the criminal law may identify types of content that cause significant harm, and would therefore fall within the scope of the regime, the criminal law does not constitute a complete list of harms against which we would expect a service provider to take action. Nor is harm caused only by content but also by the *impact of the underlying systems* such as software, business processes and their resourcing/effectiveness. We therefore do not think that the question of whether an action constitutes a criminal offence is helpful in determining harms (2019: 40, emphasis added).

Dismissing the idea that in the interests of legal and democratic legitimacy the level of harm should be specified in detail in statute, Woods and Perrin argue, instead, that 'the detail of the harms should be derived from high level statements of relevant harms by the regulator and set down in code' (ibid: 41). They also airily note that 'in our experience of regulation, competent regulators have had little difficulty in the past in working out what harm means' and add, quoting Baroness Gender on the Communications Act 2003:

> If in 2003 there was general acceptance relating to content of programmes for television and radio, protecting the public from offensive and harmful material, why have those definitions changed, or what makes them undeliverable now? Why did we understand what we meant by 'harm' in 2003 but appear to ask what it is today? (ibid).

The answer is provided by Graham Smith (2019), who points out that:

> … in 2003 the legislators did not have to understand what the vague term 'harm' meant because they gave Ofcom the power to decide. It is no surprise if Ofcom has had little difficulty, since it is in reality not 'working out what harms means' but deciding on its own meanings. It is, in effect, performing a delegated legislative function.

As noted earlier, the Communications Act refers to 'offensive and harmful' material. However, it makes no attempt to define it. Instead, in section 319(1)(h), Ofcom is charged with ensuring that 'generally accepted standards are applied to the contents of television and radio services so as to provide adequate protection for members of the public from the inclusion in such services of offensive and harmful material'. And section 319(4)(a) insists that in setting and securing these standards, Ofcom must have regard to 'the degree of harm or offence likely to be caused by the inclusion of any particular sort of material in programmes generally, or in programmes of a particular description'.

'Generally accepted standards' and 'broad public opinion'

How Ofcom operationalises these (and other) legal requirements laid down in the Act can be understood by referring to its *Broadcasting code* (2020), section two of which is entitled 'Harm and offence'. Paragraph 2.3 states that:

> In applying generally accepted standards broadcasters must ensure that material which may cause offence is justified by the context. …. Such material may include, but is not limited to, offensive language, violence, sex, sexual violence, humiliation, distress, violation of human dignity, discriminatory treatment or language (for example on the grounds of age, disability, gender reassignment, pregnancy and maternity, race, religion or belief, sex and sexual orientation, and marriage and civil partnership). Appropriate information should also be broadcast where it would assist in avoiding or minimising offence.

This part of the code also includes sections on violence, dangerous behaviour and suicide; exorcism, the occult and the paranormal; and hypnotic and other techniques, simulated news and photosensitive epilepsy.

From this, it is clear that the manner in which Ofcom has 'decided on its own meanings' of harm has considerable potential impact on a very wide range of programme content – perhaps far wider than most people realise. Of course, Ofcom, unlike its predecessors – the ITA, IBA and ITC – does not have the power to pre-censor programmes, but it most certainly has the power of post-broadcast sanction, and the vast majority of UK programme-makers know exactly what is and is not acceptable, and thus abide by Ofcom's standards. The point at which editorial judgement shades over into self-censorship is very hard to locate.

A similar point about a broad regulatory remit being granted by legislation which specifically mentions harm is the Video Recordings Act 1984. As amended in 1994, this requires the British Board of Film Classification (BBFC), when classifying videos, to have:

> … special regard … to any harm that may be caused to potential viewers or, through their behaviour, to society by the manner in which the work deals with – (a) criminal behaviour; (b) illegal drugs; (c) violent behaviour or incidents; (d) horrific behaviour or incidents; or (e) human sexual activity.

Admittedly the notion of harm here is rather more specific than in the Communications Act but, as in the case of Ofcom, it is significant that the BBFC feels that the legislation entitles it to cast the regulatory net widely. Its current *Guidelines* define harm thus:

> In relation to harm, we will consider whether the material, either on its own, or in combination with other content of a similar nature, may cause any harm at the category concerned. This includes not just any harm that may result from the behaviour of potential viewers, but also any moral or soci-

etal harm that may be caused by, for example, desensitising a potential viewer to the effects of violence, degrading a potential viewer's sense of empathy, encouraging a dehumanised view of others, encouraging anti-social attitudes, reinforcing unhealthy fantasies, or eroding a sense of moral responsibility. Especially with regard to children, harm may also include impairing social and moral development, distorting a viewer's sense of right and wrong, and limiting their capacity for compassion (2019: 7).

It could be argued, and doubtless Brian Winston would have done so, that under the aegis of preventing harm, these regulatory authorities are going beyond the bounds of what is acceptable or desirable in a democratic society. Admittedly these are not latter-day versions of Oscar Wilde's Miss Prism, for whom the mark of fiction was that the good ended happily and the bad unhappily, but they are still encroaching on broadly moral and ethical issues which some may feel should be none of their business. It might also be objected that Ofcom's 'generally accepted standards' and the BBFC's 'broad public opinion' (ibid: 7) are extremely difficult to identify and satisfy in a society as heterogeneous and diverse as our own.

New media, old problems, new laws
However, this is by no means an argument against media regulation *per se*, nor to deny that the internet has, if not created new problems in the realm of media content, then certainly greatly exacerbated already-existing ones (and not simply in the media field, either). Child abuse materials (which, it should be remembered, are the actual records of an extremely serious crime), bullying, harassment, threats, incitement to commit acts of terrorism, all can most certainly be considered as harmful in Winston's sense, and thus should be the subject of specific legislation (as, indeed, some already are). For example, if someone is bullied and then, as a direct result of that bullying, commits suicide or has a nervous breakdown, that is clearly harm by any definition. Take, for example, the harms caused by the online bullying of Caroline Criado-Perez after she had campaigned for a woman to appear on a banknote, harms which were recognised as such (albeit belatedly) by both the police and the Crown Prosecution Service and which caused two people to be charged and found guilty under section 127(1)(a) of the Communications Act, of which more below. (For further details of this case see BBC (2014) and Topping (2014)).

This is the kind of approach outlined by the Law Commission's 2021 report *Modernising communications offences*, which represents an attempt to deal with the subject of harm and offence in a more measured and nuanced way than that proposed by the White Paper and the Online Safety Bill, with their elaborate regulatory structure, sweeping scope and apparent disregard of the many dangers posed to freedom of expression by the measures which they blithely propose.

The report addresses itself, in particular, to the need to reform current laws which have been used against abusive behaviour online of one kind or another. In the commission's view, 'the existing patchwork of criminal law is unclear and has an unduly broad scope' (2021: 4). Indeed, they are 'concerned that the current offences are so broad that they could, in certain circumstances, interfere disproportionately with the right to freedom of expression protected under Article 10 of the ECHR' (ibid). They also make it clear that their aim is 'to modernise the framework of criminal offences that target communications and ensure only sufficiently harmful communications are criminalised' and, in doing so, 'to ensure our recommendations do not extend inappropriately the reach of the existing communications offences or overlap significantly with other crimes' (ibid).

The commission is particularly exercised by two offences. The first concerns Section 1 of the Malicious Communications Act 1988, which makes it a criminal offence to send someone, by any means, a message which is indecent, grossly offensive, a threat, or false, and if the purpose of sending the message was to cause 'distress or anxiety' to the recipient. The second is the above-mentioned section 127(1)(a) of the Communications Act 2003, which criminalises the sending, via a 'public electronic communications network', of a message which is 'grossly offensive or of an indecent, obscene or menacing character'. The commission argues that:

> Reliance on vague terms like 'grossly offensive' and 'indecent' raises concerns that the offences criminalise some forms of free expression that ought to be protected. Simply put, these adjectives do not always correspond to harm. For example, consensual sexting between adults could be 'indecent', but is not obviously worthy of criminalisation (ibid: 6).

On the other hand, however, the commission also feels that offences do not always effectively target the harms arising from online abuse, because too often the threshold of criminality is set too low.

From categories of content to the consequences of communication

The commission seeks to address these problems by shifting away from assessing categories of content, such as 'indecent' or 'grossly offensive', to assessing the consequences of communication in cases where these can be defined as harmful. But whilst bearing in mind that online abuse is one of the major challenges for the current law, the commission is keen to stress that it has 'tried not to constrain the offences to particular forms of communication', so that they 'do not arbitrarily criminalise communications differently based on the mode of communication' (ibid: 8).

Turning to specifics, the commission sets out the details of a new offence based on likely psychological harm to replace the offences in the Acts noted above. This, it contends, 'will more effectively protect freedom of expression and avoid over-criminalisation while better targeting the myriad types of harmful communications' (ibid: 9). Briefly, this offence would be committed by someone who sends a communication that is deliberately intended to cause harm to a likely audience, with harm being defined here as psychological harm amounting at least to serious distress. When deciding whether such a communication was likely to cause harm to its likely audience, a court would have to have regard to the context in which the communication was sent, including the characteristics of the likely recipient or recipients (ibid: 7).

The commission also proposes a new offence involving threatening communications. Here the defendant would be liable if they sent – by any means – a communication that conveys a threat of serious harm, and if, in conveying the threat, they intended its object to fear that it would be carried out, or was reckless as to whether they would fear that this would happen. For the purposes of this offence, serious harm would include serious injury (amounting to grievous bodily harm as understood under the Offences Against the Person Act 1861), rape and serious financial harm (ibid: 13).

Conclusion

Brian Winston might well have regarded the Law Commission's definitions of what constitute harmful forms of communication as still pushing too far beyond the perceptible and verifiable. But one feels that at least he would have welcomed its attempt to define what it means by harm in relation to certain specific offences and that he would have endorsed its media-neutral approach which stresses that what is illegal offline is also illegal online – something which is all too often forgotten or ignored in endless jeremiads against the evils of the online world. These are a particular speciality of sections of Britain's national press which, of course, have their own reasons for advocating the censorship of those areas of the internet which they do not own and control. Yet this has led such doughty enemies of the 'nanny state' and 'red tape' to argue for and endorse a measure such as the Online Safety Bill (from which, of course, they have successfully lobbied to exempt themselves) – an act of arrant hypocrisy remarkable by even their debased standards.

References

Article 19 (2019) *Freedom of expression in the UK: Policy briefing*. Available online at https://www.article19.org/wp-content/uploads/2020/03/Fex_UK_briefing.pdf, accessed on 2 September 2021

BBC News (2014) Two guilty over abusive tweets to Caroline Criado-Perez, 7 January. Available online at https://www.bbc.co.uk/news/uk-25641941, accessed on 2 September 2021

British Board of Film Classification (2019) *Classification guidelines*. Available online at file:///C:/Users/owner/Downloads/bbfc-classification-guidelines%20(1).pdf, accessed on 2 September 2021.

Department for Digital, Culture, Media and Sport/Home Office (2019) *Online Harms White Paper*. Available online at https://assets.publishing.service.gov.uk/government/uploads/system/uploads/attachment_data/file/944310/Online_Harms_White_Paper_Full_Government_Response_to_the_consultation_CP_354_CCS001_CCS1220695430-001__V2.pdf, accessed on 2 September 2021

Department for Digital, Culture, Media and Sport/Home Office (2020) *Online Harms White Paper: Full government response to the consultation*. Available online at https://www.gov.uk/government/consultations/online-harms-white-paper/outcome/online-harms-white-paper-full-government-response, accessed on 2 September 2021

Department for Digital, Culture, Media and Sport/Home Office (2021) *The Online Safety Bill: Impact assessment*. Available online at https://assets.publishing.service.gov.uk/government/uploads/system/uploads/attachment_data/file/985283/Draft_Online_Safety_Bill_-_Impact_Assessment_Web_Accessible.pdf, accessed on 2 September 2021

Index on Censorship (2019) Online harms proposals pose serious risks to freedom of expression, 8 April. Available online at https://www.indexoncensorship.org/2019/04/online-harms-proposals-pose-serious-risks-to-freedom-of-expression-online/, accessed on 2 September 2012

Law Commission (2021) *Modernising communications offences: Summary of the final report*. Available online at https://s3-eu-west-2.amazonaws.com/lawcom-prod-storage-11jsxou24uy7q/uploads/2021/07/Summary-of-Modernising-Communications-Offences-2021.pdf, accessed on 2 September 2021

Mill, John Stuart (1985 [1859]) *On liberty*, London, Penguin Books

Ofcom (2020) *Broadcasting code*. Available online at https://www.ofcom.org.uk/tv-radio-and-on-demand/broadcast-codes/broadcast-code, accessed on 2 September 2021

Julian Petley

Open Rights Group (2019) *ORG policy responses to Online Harms White Paper*, May. Available online at https://modx.openrightsgroup.org/assets/files/reports/report_pdfs/ORG_Policy_Lines_Online_Harms_WP.pdf, accessed on 2 September 2021

Smith, Graham (2019) Users behaving badly – the Online Harms White Paper, *Cyberleagle*, 18 April. Available online at https://www.cyberleagle.com/2019/04/users-behaving-badly-online-harms-white.html, accessed on 2 September 2021

Smith, Graham (2020) The Online Harms edifice takes shape, *Cyberleagle*, 17 December. Available online at https://www.cyberleagle.com/2020/12/the-online-harms-edifice-takes-shape.html, accessed on 2 September 2021

Smith, Graham (2021) Harm version 3.0: The draft Online Safety Bill, *Cyberleagle*, 16 May. Available online at https://www.cyberleagle.com/2021/05/harm-version-30-draft-online-safety-bill.html, accessed on 2 September 2021

Topping, Alexandra (2014) Jane Austen Twitter row: Two plead guilty to abusive tweets, 7 January. Available online at https://www.theguardian.com/society/2014/jan/07/jane-austen-banknote-abusive-tweets-criado-perez, accessed 2 September 2021

Winston, Brian (2005) *Messages: Free expression, media and the West from Gutenberg to Google*, London and New York, Routledge

Winston, Brian (2014) *The Rushdie fatwa and after*, Basingstoke, Palgrave Macmillan

Woods, Lorna and Perrin, William (2019) *Online harm reduction – a statutory duty of care and regulator*, Carnegie UK Trust. Available online at https://d1ssu070pg2v9i.cloudfront.net/pex/pex_carnegie2021/2019/04/06084627/Online-harm-reduction-a-statutory-duty-of-care-and-regulator.pdf

Note on the contributor

Julian Petley is Emeritus and Honorary Professor of Journalism at Brunel University London. The second edition of his *Culture wars: The media and the British Left* (with James Curran and Ivor Gaber) was published by Routledge in 2019. He is a member of the editorial board of the *British Journalism Review* and the principal editor of the *Journal of British Cinema and Television*. A former journalist, he contributes to online publications such as *Inforrm*, *Byline Times* and *openDemocracy*.

PAPER

Pratāp Rughani

Towards restorative narrative

This paper argues for an experiment in bringing together moving image and mediation practices to create a more relational media – socially designed and biased enough to nurture the connective tissue between communities, drawing on practices from restorative justice including deep listening and searching for shades of grey. Meanwhile, swathes of social and mass media are increasingly polarised. Key production processes and financial structures feed this trend, magnifying the attitudes and algorithms that lean towards conflict. This trend hollows out the quality or sometimes the prospect of dialogue in the public sphere and threatens to break the connective tissue that forms the habitus of UK multi-cultures. In response to these issues, the paper suggests some strategies to refuse and reverse toxic polarisation. It argues that the need for participatory and community media is stronger than ever and asks: what is needed to create meetings and media to build creative explorations that nurture empathic understanding, especially when we disagree? Finally, can the processes of restorative justice offer a model for 'restorative narrative' that could frame a new media genre of storytelling designed to build mutual understanding and connection that obtains on either side of emotive issues whether or not we agree.

Keywords: restorative narrative, polarisation, mass media, ethics

Introduction
Mass media journalism typically presents words, images, rushes and stories by grasping, heightening and juxtaposing tension and differences. This suits (and is shaped by) a news storytelling culture that privileges black-and-white clashes of current or coming conflict. The bias leans towards the dramatic, serving audiences that mostly expect and reliably consume this dynamic to 'make sense' of a far more complex world.

These dynamics are recently joined, supported and extended by swathes of social media that blur distinctions between fact and editorial comment, further enabled by the now commonplace rendering of disinformation in the texture of communications. Today, far too much of our mixed media landscape can be characterised by 'toxic polarisation' (Coleman 2021). Whilst liberal democracies are familiar with articulating threats to 'free speech', they are less practised in reflecting on and counteracting the insidious effects of speech untethered from community values or a connecting vision. This primes the landscape for a culture of polarisation to flourish.

In 'old media', this dynamic was already problematic. I quickly found in my work in print, radio and television current affairs that the compression necessary for short sound-bites and 'punchy' headlines meant that shades of grey were better explored elsewhere, some distance from the news agenda. I settled on longer-form documentary practices.

Across thirty years, in many places and with people facing conflict or its aftermath, I have listened closely to and reported on the aftermath of atrocity, sometimes engaging disparate arguments on different sides of an event, idea or issue. In South Africa, Rwanda, Aboriginal Australia, the UK and elsewhere I have tried to explore counter-arguments with each side in the search for understandings for diverse audiences, conceiving documentary film as a kind of arena in which many experiences can unfold, with enough open space for an audience to make sense of competing perceptions and experiences and settle on their own view. Today I wonder if this is enough. Rather than mirroring reality, too much media risks further damaging the situations it purports to describe, leaving a more polarised trail for audiences and uncomfortable but necessary questions for practitioners (Rughani 2010: 169).

I'm about to make an argument for an experiment in bringing together film and mediation practices to rethink the information architecture for a more relational media – socially designed to be biased enough to nurture the connective tissue *between* communities, drawing on practices from restorative justice including deep listening and searching for shades of grey. In making the case, it's important to underline the essential work of robust and rigorous re-

Pratăp Rughani

porting and its significance, for example in exposing crime, corruption and holding officials to account. Errol Morris's film *The thin blue line* (1988) was both a stylistic innovation in documentary practice and is widely credited with securing the release from prison of Randall Adams who had been convicted for a murder he did not commit. Morris urges that documentary innovation should not be marked by a retreat into partiality and implicitly cautions against the solipsistic dangers of relativism:

> To those who argue that there's no such thing as objective truth, I say ask a man strapped in an electric chair who says 'I didn't do it' ... forgive me there is such a thing as truth – the truth (Morris 2011).

The argument here is not about 'objectivity' or the importance of investigative journalism or the inevitable 'black-and-white' aspects of the fourth estate. Rather it is a response to the reflex polarisation of media cultures and the risk of public scepticism turning further towards cynicism, with consequences for social cohesion in diverse communities where the work of creating and recreating dialogue in UK multicultures is fragile and, by turns, contested.

Tipping points

It is widely documented how voting is fuelled by playing on fear of the 'outsider', stereotypes and bigotry, such as that seeded by Russian bots. Their pivotal effect in fuelling the 'alt right' has already tipped many elections. In 2018, the UK Electoral Commission found the Vote Leave campaign guilty of breaking electoral law, referring them to the National Crime Agency for investigation. In May 2020, police confirmed that no action would be taken. Pro-Brexit campaigns paid £3.5 million to AggregateIQ (AIQ) to collect and analyse people's data in order to personalise fake political slogans – for example, to spread the lie that Turkey was about to join the EU, to whip up and channel racialised fear. Dominic Cummings, Vote Leave's director, boasted on AIQ's website: 'Without a doubt, the Vote Leave campaign owes a great deal of its success to the work of AggregateIQ. We couldn't have done it without them.'

How can storytelling travel a wiser route to enable open discussion that might withstand visceral prejudices? Just ten years ago, Wael Ghonim's Facebook page was widely credited as a catalyst for the Tahrir Square demonstrations that marked the brief Arab Spring in Cairo in 2011. The web enabled freer speech but that season, in Egypt, ended in military intervention, a coup and the return to dictatorship in all but name. Ghonim later re-evaluated social media, disturbed by its reckless use by populists, activists and dictators. He fled Egypt and later co-founded a new social media platform, Parlio, that included a civility pledge and used real names. 'We're here to learn new perspectives; not to win arguments,' the platform said. Trolling was forbidden and 'expanding horizons' privileged.

Parlio developed from Ghonim's question: how to design social media experiences to nurture thoughtfulness, civility or quality of engagement? Assessment of such aspirations is overdue (especially since Parlio was bought by Quora in March 2016). Are my 'likes' the reward for agreement with a view floating on the surface that suits another's preconception rather than a deeper engagement with ideas? Where are the algorithms and metrics that reward us for rethinking, changing our minds even, rather than approving our own echo?

For all their benefits, the deep shadows of social media platforms are increasingly apparent, yet it's taking far too long for Twitter and Facebook, especially, to deliver or enforce a robust ethical framework or act meaningfully on existing policies to quickly and reliably screen out abuse or disinformation. National governments appear at a loss to apply the norms expected of broadcast media, despite these channels' significant experience of navigating the tensions between 'free speech' and 'hate speech'.

Meanwhile, the profits of online vitriol are not properly taxed and the platforms' income generation model rewards a lucrative trade in the heat and friction of polarisation, weakening and even denaturing the very tissue that holds a culture together.

Documentary: Promoting a more relational, participatory approach

The flourishing of an easy trade in bigotry-fuelled conflict online reminds me of Leni Riefenstahl's riposte fifty years after making *Triumph of the will* (1935), her striking documentary, commissioned by Hitler, introducing him to film audiences and featuring the Nazi Nuremberg rallies of 1934. Riefenstahl maintained that it did not matter what the Nazi speeches she featured were about: 'Whether it was about politics or vegetables or fruit, I couldn't give a damn. ... To me the film was not about politics, it was an event. ...' What does political responsibility mean? And to whom is one responsible? Riefenstahl wanted to make a 'great' film, to hell with the consequences.

Ray Müller's flirtatious rapport and the careful documentary interview technique he used in the making of The wonderful, horrible life of Leni Riefenstahl (1993) encouraged Riefenstahl to speak out on these issues. In Müller's admirable and long documentary (188 mins), his relational approach revealed more of Riefenstahl than his subject intended. In shorter works, too, the directed camera can 'see', revealing to audiences things that are easily overlooked when a priori ideas stand in the way of what is in front of our eyes. The ability to be alive to nuance is essential here, flourishing in documentary's observational modes, if a space can be configured to loosen pre-conceived story structures and open out on other ways of looking.

When shooting Justine (Lotus Films 2013),[1] about a young woman who rarely speaks, I made an 'anti-journalistic' choice to avoid naming the principal character's neurological condition, as I was concerned that if she were introduced in terms of her medical history, it might keep her sealed in a box (an audience's idea of 'neurological disorder' for example) from which she might not escape. This was arguably a strange choice but I was concerned that when most media engage with people with disabilities, the disability or 'condition' is the 'newsworthy' fact. The risk is that such reportage collapses the individual into her diagnosis and eclipses the person herself.

Is a different kind of communication possible through a more relational, participatory approach where stories emerge 'with' and 'alongside' rather than simply 'about' the other? Pioneering Vietnamese video artist Trinh T. Minh-ha describes her aspiration in moving image practice as restoring proximity of the subject and recognising the place of subjectivity:

In the context of power relations, speaking for, about, and on behalf of is very different from speaking with and nearby ... what has to be given up first and foremost is the voice of omniscient knowledge (Hohenberger 2008: 118-119).

Close listening when making Justine helped my direction and camerawork be led by shifts in her emotional temperature and small happenings. Configuring this space brought changes that re-formed the narrative so that a new visual journey emerged, that is more led by Justine's experience and decisions. The 'advanced neurological disorder' and 'autism' labels typically led to a pathology of Justine suggesting that it would be very difficult for her to show empathy – either cognitive or affective. Yet close attention to Justine revealed (and possibly facilitated) her clearly empathic responses recorded on camera in several situations.

Freed of the medical labels, it was easier to observe and film, and on showing a fine-cut to her family, her mother paused to say: 'God. I never thought she would do that,' when observing a sequence in which Justine was able to anticipate other children's needs and take initiative to help them by opening a gate.

Likewise, audiences started to hear and see aspects of Justine that undercut conventional expectations. Justine could start to emerge (I speculate) more on her own terms, rather than those of conventional media interest, that typically frames and reduces her to her 'disabilities'.[2]

When storytelling, it's important to ask: how do the subjects of these stories benefit from their involvement and who else benefits? Despite Justine's micro-budget, interest in the film on the educational and film festival screenings

PAPER

Justine opening a gate: A still from the film, Justine (photograph by Pratāp Rughani and Wakulenko)

Pratāp Rughani

circuit generated income. That money went to Justine and supported some leisure interests, so she has seen direct benefits in her life. Payments should be carefully agreed to avoid the dangers of 'cheque-book journalism' but it is also time to offer a new transparency in the financial flows of productions and ensure that the main participants see real rewards.

Finding an audience
Films such as *Justine* found audiences at film festivals, community screenings and galleries. Leading UK gallery spaces, so recently uninterested in promoting documentaries, are now replete with them as audiences respond to socially-engaged art. Here, the storytelling can be less circumscribed and offer a more open encounter. Media in gallery spaces can experiment with other ways of seeing. A retreat from broadcast and mass media, however, risks reducing work to bourgeois entertainment, ultimately decorative in its setting, whilst mainstream and social media bifurcate into mutually enforcing bubbles.

Even the making of mainstream broadcast documentary still struggles to resist the gravitational pull to exaggerate and heighten differences and to keep attention through ad-breaks – sometimes seriously distorting information in the search for the most 'compelling' narrative. Some documentaries tip into becoming more openly partisan and adversarial media. Yet this adversarial posture undermines the potential to find a common ground that can nurture the kind of trust to renew connection through an exploration of difference. That connection can be within tantalising reach since, underneath the culture clashes of 'identity politics', groups professing mutual loathing often find that there is much more that they agree on.[3]

In today's age of Trumpian tweets, the racism (among other hatreds) is brazen and normalised. But Hannah Arendt reminds us that the totalitarian impulse is not the property of a single political complexion (Arendt 1958).

Attractors
Views are triggered and easily congeal. Why? Professor Peter Coleman, of Columbia University's Center for Cooperation and Conflict Resolution, leads a research centre whose studies conclude that the neurology of intractable polarisation is producing a hard-wired response through 'attractors' that are hard to shift. Our brain's amygdala is activated by fear and much of social media's platform engineering triggers these responses. As Coleman et al. argue (2005):

Attractors, in short, channel mental and behavioural experience into a narrow range of malignant (but coherent) states. Attempting to move the system out of its attractor promotes forces that reinstate the system at its attractor. This means that attempts to change the state of conflict without changing the mechanisms that continually reinstate the conflict are likely to be futile, resulting only in short-term changes. To promote lasting change, it is necessary to change the attractor states of the system. This is no easy feat, since it is tantamount to changing the mechanisms responsible for the system's dynamics.

Is it possible, however, that with the right support, attractors could be supported to drive virtuous, rather than just vicious circles?

Design for dialogue
Journalism's production and editorial guidelines have arguably a bigger sector-wide role to play at this juncture, when under-regulated media grow a culture of advanced polarisation and hate speech flourishes. Facebook's tilt towards 'neo-Nazi shopfronts' is tracked in the Center for Countering Digital Hate's publication *Hatebook* (see counterhate.com/hatebook). Moreover, enforcement of the National Union of Journalists' Code of Conduct[4] and ethics guidelines, broadcasters' editorial guidelines and regulatory frameworks to map out responsible media spaces is needed (Rughani 2013: 101-105).

Significantly, some small alternatives are emerging from grass-roots local groups such as the community-owned Bristol Cable,[5] founded in 2014, that re-centres the social context stories live in and return to. Initiatives such as Tortoise Media[6] embrace 'slow news' as an approach to distil depth from the continuing flow of superficial news updates. Both invite more participatory news values.

Dialogue and listening that privilege the space to reflect and reconsider could lead us to change our minds and escape the 'gravitational pull' of attractors. In my documentary practice, I have been fortunate to be present when people determined to pursue a vision or ideal of reconnection decide to make something better from our divisions. I have seen this unfold in entrenched conflicts, such as at the Truth and Reconciliation Commission hearings of the new South Africa for Channel 4 in 1998; the evolution of a new police service in Northern Ireland in 2004, and among London students from many diverse ethnic backgrounds decrying Islamophobia (2001 to the present).

I have also seen it fail when the conditions for good faith in listening on each side were not developed, for example at the Aboriginal Reconciliation Convention, in Australia, in 1997, when the then-Prime Minister, John Howard, reduced the history of indigenous genocide to a 'blemish' and hectored his Aboriginal audience with the pride settler Australians feel in their nation-building. There followed an extraordinary moment. With an invisible signal, the bulk of the Aboriginal audience quietly stood, remained listening, then slowly turned their backs on Howard. It was a moment that called for statesmanship with a Prime Minister standing for the wider community beyond their own partisan interests. Instead, Howard became yet more shrill, rattled through his notes and left without discussing or listening to any Aboriginal speakers.[8]

It was a profoundly disappointing and shocking moment but it did not surprise many indigenous survivors whose dignity in attending remained an unseen, unwanted gift. A recent report indicates that as many as 500 Aboriginal and Torres Strait Islander people have died in custody in Australia in the thirty years since a royal commission gave recommendations aimed at preventing indigenous deaths in the justice system, disfiguring an Australia where black lives have yet to really matter (Allam 2021).

A culture is clearly needed to reinforce a different form of communication that privileges empathy, connection and the development of a deeper confidence to make space for another's experience. In that space of listening, compassion can grow, even in extreme situations.

How to curate spaces and discussions that enable such journeys? What in our communication privileges the softening of conviction and the quieter confidence to doubt and enable another's experience to influence us? Can documentary makers be struck by how the 'storifying' of life can be richer and more interesting than the *a priori* narratives that often deliver journalists and filmmakers to a place of difficulty or conflict? How can the door to the dialogic be opened?

Modelling this approach is key. A recent BBC project, built on research into 'humanbecoming', suggests this useful, tested methodology (Kasriel 2020):

- Ask your speaker to explain their perspective and why they feel so strongly. Listen, without interruption, putting aside judgements, counter-arguments and solutions.
- Summarise the core of what you have heard and check you have understood correctly, including the emotions and texture of their story. This does not mean you have to agree.
- Ask whether they agree with your summary. If not, ask them to explain more.
- Continue with this process till the speaker gives a resounding 'Yes.' They should at this point be likely to listen to your side of the story.

The spirit of this is receptivity rather than agreement. Agreement may not follow. The point is not to agree or persuade through duress but to experience relatedness that may unsettle each other's convictions and open new channels of communication and affect. If receptivity suffuses our listening, answers may emerge, perfumed with similar qualities. NPR broadcaster Krista Tippett, in *The art of generous listening* (2019), explains how her radio series, *On being*, strives to create understanding for how another thinks. Tippett suggests we look more to 'how' and 'why', rather than 'what' and 'when' as keys to developing dialogue. By shifting our attention we expand the foundations of relatedness to focus on what truly matters, she says, and we can develop 'discernment'. 'The point is not to agree but to come into relationship. What we have in common are our questions.'

Designing for dialogue may begin as a response to political polarisation, but its effects are joyfully unpredictable. Exploring such questions will likely be profoundly inter-disciplinary. For all the advances of the West's Enlightenment, our scholarship risks being imprisoned in its own specialisms. In the face of complex challenges, the weakness of trying to tackle big questions in separate compartments is clear. Preparing the ground by learning to listen and the creativity of dialogic encounters should lead us to rethink not just why we got here but to imagine something finer.

Restorative narrative

Reflecting on many years of documentary practice with an emphasis on production ethics, the central question for me is now: how can the dynamic affordances of interactive and social media be harnessed for a different kind of storytelling, rooted in production practices of deeper listening and a rigorous search for what connects us – what we have in common, rather than the easy reflex of reacting to opposing views? With that commitment to shared community, how can documentary and other media practices engage difference better? Instead of feeding the easy heat of triggering reflex reactions, can storytellers invent media that aims to restore relationship, understanding and connection – a media that truly mediates between us?

What might success look like in this context? As with restorative justice approaches and some forms of mediation, a key focus is on creating the conditions for deeper attention, rather than attempting to cajole others into a surface agreement that may prove counterproductive. A key to unlocking polarised and apparently intractable conflict is a shift towards acceptance of the other. The work of philosopher Emmanuel Lévinas is useful here, especially his insistence on meeting the gaze of the other and the foundational ethics of cultivating this kind of attention (Hand 1989).

Some remarkable examples of the journalism that embodies this approach are collected from the edges of human endurance in the work of the Forgiveness Project[7] and the work of its founder Marina Cantacuzino. Her essay 'As mysterious as love' emphasises the cross-currents of feeling and insight where polarisation and hatred can give way to release (not necessarily forgiveness) in a jagged journey that is ultimately about reconciliation with experience and with oneself: 'Making peace with a painful event is what allows people to live with hurt and catastrophe, find resolution and move on' (Cantacuzino 2015: 12). Reconciliatory stories are hard to surface – in situations of trauma even the questions can be very hard to approach. Marian Partington, whose younger sister Lucy was a victim of the serial killers Fred and Rosemary West, eventually came to ask how she could help perpetrators to become free of the pain that led them to cause harm in the first place. Her insight gave direction and the journey of her grief unfolds just the kind of delicate journey whose deeper strength is hard to recognise – or sometimes even to understand – in cultures of oppositional storytelling (Partington 2016).

The fragile beginnings of structured support for a change in approach from media makers may be emerging. In 2013, Images and Voices of Hope developed the genre of restorative narrative 'proposing that by following the arc of recovery instead of focusing exclusively on traumatizing events, victims and the helplessness that follows, they could help build capacity in the communities they serve'.[8] Now merged with the Peace Studio, the initiative offers space for 'reflective practice' to support a shift in awareness to help practitioners configure this newer trajectory in storytelling. The resulting stories can open audiences to our own (sometimes small) restorations with things we may find 'unforgivable'. Stories of reconnected communities become tangible by tilting production ethics to seek narratives that privilege listening, exchange and shared concerns. Stories that chart and document collective commitment to a dynamic of exchange might then lead to reconnection or 'restorative narrative' as a recognised strand of media production. The prize here is not necessarily agreement on an issue between formally polarised people but enough of a convergence of experience for mutual understanding of the other. Indeed, stories of restoration of connection can model that possibility to others. If we see such stories regularly in our media, they become a more tangible possibility.

Conclusion: Re-conceiving media as ethically responsible

Can a story production process now emerge that re-conceives media as ethically responsible 'connective tissue' to configure a public space to enable storytellers, subjects and audiences to understand and come into relationship with others' diverging perspectives? Achieving this means letting go of the pretence of a *priori* pseudo-objectivity. In their article 'Racism, hate speech, and social media: A systematic review and critique', Matamoros-Fernández and Farkas (2020: 218) note: 'There is a preponderance of research on racism, hate speech, and social media done by white scholars that rarely acknowledges the positionality of the authors, which risks reinforcing colour-blind ideologies within the field.'

Recognising our 'positionality' by developing a reflexive awareness is a significant move in creating an environment that can reach beyond a single perspective towards a deeper pluralism. This paradox remains a challenge for many media practitioners. Many of us like to think that we are 'impartial' or that we have already escaped the gravitational pull of our own conditioning, when the idea that we are already free of our biases can be the very blinkers that reduce our ability to recognise how our limitations may invisibly structure our thinking and storytelling. The humbling recognition of our limitations, along with the work that flows in building teams to research broader perspectives, can map out a new alchemy in storytelling.

Just as some natural history programming features a 'making of' section that unpacks the technical triumphs and hardships, could a 'story lab' sidebar or section of a restorative article or programme reveal the restorative work that enables the prospect of reconnection and community forged from diverse perspectives? If the medium can become the message, what if the process of creating that media is dedicated to restoring relationships through the light of understanding difference – inventing an avowedly restorative media? What new visions may then flow from these new narratives and the ethics of such a media practice?

Notes

[1] Film (and debate) available online at https://ethics.arts.ac.uk/

[2] For an exploration of the approach to storytelling taken here and the foundational ethical questions that underpin this trajectory, see Ethics for making, by Pratāp Rughani and Iris Wakulenko (2020). Available online at https://screenworks.org.uk/archive/volume-10-2/ethics-for-making

[3] See https://www.theguardian.com/politics/2021/nov/17/voters-in-west-divided-more-by-identity-than-issues-survey-finds, accessed on 26 November 2021

[4] https://www.nuj.org.uk/about-us/rules-and-guidance/code-of-conduct.html, accessed on 21 November 2021

[5] https://thebristolcable.org/, accessed on 20 November 2021

[6] https://www.tortoisemedia.com/, accessed on 25 November 2021

[7] https://www.theforgivenessproject.com/, accessed on 29 November 2021

[8] https://thepeacestudio.org/, accessed on 27 November 2021

References

Allam, L. (2021) 'Beyond heartbreaking': 500 Indigenous deaths in custody since 1991 royal commission, *Guardian*, 6 December. Available online at https://www.theguardian.com/australia-news/2021/dec/06/beyond-heartbreaking-500-indigenous-deaths-in-custody-since-1991-royal-commission, accessed on 7 December 2021

Arendt, H. (1958) *The origins of totalitarianism*, New York, Meridian Books

Cantacuzino, M. (2015) *The Forgiveness Project: Stories for a vengeful age*, London: Jessica Kingsley, second edition

Coleman, P., Vallacher, R. R., Nowak, A. and Ngoc, L. B. (2005) Intractable conflict as an attractor: Presenting a dynamical model of conflict, escalation, and intractability, *SSRN Electronic Journal*, Vol. 50. Available online at DOI: 10.2139/ssrn.734963

Coleman, P. (2021) *The way out: How to overcome toxic polarisation*, New York, Columbia University Press

Hand, S. (ed.) (1989) *The Lévinas reader*, Oxford, Basil Blackwell

Hohenberger, E. (2008) Vietnam/USA: Trinh T. Minh-ha in an interview, Pearce, G. and McLaughlin, C. (eds) *Truth or dare: Art and documentary*, Bristol, Intellect Books pp 104-121

Kasriel, E. (2020) Deep listening: Finding common ground with opponents, BBC News, 4 March. Available online at https://www.bbc.co.uk/news/health-51705369

Morris, E. (2011) Annual BAFTA David Lean lecture: Investigating with the camera. Available online at https://www.bafta.org/media-centre/press-releases/errol-morris-delivers-the-2011-bafta-david-lean-lecture, accessed on 8 December 2021

Matamoros-Fernández, A. and Farkas, J. (2021) Racism, hate speech, and social media: A systematic review and critique, *Television & New Media*, Vol. 22, No. 2. Available online at https://doi.org/10.1177/1527476420982230, accessed on 7 December 2021

Müller, R. (1993) *The wonderful, horrible life of Leni Riefenstahl*. Available online at https://learningonscreen.ac.uk/ondemand/index.php/prog/004ACA50?bcast=2766017, accessed on 24 May 2020

Partington, M. (2016) *If you sit very still*, London, Jessica Kingsley

Rughani, P. (2010) Are you a vulture? Reflecting on the ethics and aesthetics of atrocity coverage and its aftermath, Keeble, R. L., Tulloch, J. and Zollmann, F. (eds) (2010) *Peace journalism, war and conflict resolution*, New York, Peter Lang pp 157-172

Rughani, P. (2013) The dance of documentary ethics, Winston, B. (ed.) *The BFI documentary film book*, London, Palgrave Macmillan pp 98-109

Tippett, K. (2019) *The art of generous living*. Available online at https://www.youtube.com/watch?v=J5W36VWNd9E, accessed on 30 November 2021

Note on the contributor

Dr Pratāp Rughani is Director of Lotus Films and Professor of Documentary Practices at the University of the Arts London, where he is Head of Research at the London College of Communications. He is a documentary-maker with a particular interest in how film can help create the conditions for inter-cultural communication. He is a trustee of Pragya and the Karuna Trust, NGOs working in the UK and India for social and environmental justice. He feels a debt of gratitude and appreciation for Professor Brian Winston and, following his death, would like to pay tribute to his thoughtful leadership and academic insight over decades. The path to deeper reflection is ever-inspired by Thea Ellora. See https://www.arts.ac.uk/research/ual-staff-researchers/pratap-rughani and http://www.lotusfilms.co.uk.

TRIBUTE

John Mair

'Praxis personified: He didn't just talk media, he made it'

Brian Winston was a true polymath – able to talk and write on a vast range of subjects. His intellectual *piste* was large and deep.

Brian wrote for several of my curated book collections – on the BBC, on the pandemic and other topics. Always original. You gave him an idea – though usually it was the other way round – and he would run with it, put it through his institutional memory and wide reading and deliver before the deadline. The angles he came up with were startling – debating whether the BBC was really 100 years old in 2022 or the centenary should really be 2027 when the British Broadcasting Company morphed to the Corporation. He was probably right – in which case the BBC is wasting lots of money this year on the wrong date. In another essay, he asked whether the BBC should abandon news!

On the Covid-19 pandemic, too, he was also unique. He actually wrote a chapter for one of my books in his hospital bed with drips going into him. Brian being Brian was fighting the doctors to let him out. They did eventually but the last few years he was not in the best of health. He even delivered a lecture on Zoom to a conference of the Association for Journalism Education from a ward wearing his hospital gown.

Brian was praxis personified: he didn't just talk media, he made it, starting with his first job in that ITV talent factory Granada as a producer on the esteemed *World in Action* in 1963. From current affairs to documentaries and winning a National Emmy in 1985.

That curiosity, narrative skill and mischief-making of a good producer came in useful on his transfer to the academe. He left the small screen for the intellectual groves of Glasgow. The book *Bad News*, in 1976, paved the way for hard-hitting media research. The cases for bias made by a simple analysis of output. Brian was a founder member of the Glasgow University Media Group which produced that and subsequent volumes. Their effect on newsroom practice was significant. People started to examine their in-built biases and a new genre of media research was born.

He went on to take up prominent positions at the universities of New York, Penn State, Cardiff and Westminster. It would be kind to say that bureaucracy and academic politics were not his métier. Eventually, the new University of Lincoln beckoned.

Once again he went on to widen his field of interest to include freedom of speech, the meaning of documentaries and much more. It was no accident that Lincoln made him The Lincoln Professor in 2007. From his lair in the shadow of the cathedral he continued to think and write widely – 20 books on subjects from media, technology and society, to John Grierson, to fake news. He was the thinking person's thinker.

On a personal level he was always very kind. Once at a party in the Lincolnshire Wolds my wife and I knew nobody but he made a great effort to come across and talk to us for a long time.

He made us feel at home.

I will miss his intellect and his friendship.

John Mair is a former BBC, ITV and Channel 4 producer. He taught at several universities in the UK and aboard and has edited 46 books on media matters. Brian Winston contributed to four of those on the BBC – and on other topics. Published by Abramis Academic and Bite-Sized books, all are available on Amazon.

TRIBUTE

Ivor Gaber

'Proud, paid-up member of the awkward squad'

It's no doubt been said many times before but Brian Winston was truly 'a force of nature' – never more so than when demonstrating to journalist colleagues on the editorial board of the British Journalism Review that media academics were not 'out to get them' and really did know a thing or two about the media. Brian was an active member of the board and, despite his deteriorating health, thanks to Zoom, continued to be so. I have very fond memories of his entering debates that were beginning to feel slightly sterile and, from what looked like a rather left field position, gradually, through the depth of his historical knowledge and his sheer erudition, steering the discussion into more productive areas (usually).

There can be few academics who can claim to have identified the central role of fake news and falsehood (the currently fashionable term for lying) in modern mass communications as effectively, and as early, as Brian. From Lies, damn lies and documentaries, in 2000, to The roots of fake news: Objecting to objective journalism 20 years later (written with his son, Matthew, now following in Brian's academic footsteps) he has seen 'truth telling' – a term which neither Brian nor I would be comfortable with – as central to the business of communications. Of course, the very sub-title of his latest book indicates that Brian was no starry-eyed romantic believing in the simple pursuit of 'truth', nor was he a wilfully myopic post-modernist arguing for the relativism of everything. In short, Brian was a proud, paid-up member of the awkward squad (no, make that the commanding officer), consisting of those who refuse to be pigeon-holed around this crucial topic – a squad to which I also claim membership.

Brian's refusal to be pigeon-holed, and his absolute commitment to factuality and the historical method, were never more in evidence than in his trenchant contributions to the sometimes heated (but always amicable) discussions at the British Journalism Review – an admirable publication that seeks to bring journalists and academics together to write, publish and argue. The academics would nod sagely as Brian explained the centrality of Vlad the Impaler to the origins of fake news, whilst the journalists – initially exchanging cynical glances – would eventually become entranced as Brian continued to weave magical, but scholarly, tales.

In my own academic trajectory I was a long-term Winston fan. From his perceptive deconstruction and criticism of techno-determinism to his last mission to give the 'fake news' debate a more sophisticated analytical and historical context, Brian was a powerful influence on both academics and practitioners alike, ranging from would-be journalists fresh out of university to the most esteemed documentary-makers – all recognising their debt to Brian's copious contributions to the discipline.

From my own various academic resting places, I have observed Brian enviously as an academic entrepreneur par excellence – a friendly but tough 'competitor'. And I have had the pleasure of witnessing Brian's contributions at academic conferences where his papers were always worth attending, not just for their invariably challenging, and frequently groundbreaking, content but also for his lively style of presentation.

Both Brian and I came out of professional broadcast journalism to find ourselves wandering in the unfamiliar groves of academe. Brian's background on Granada TV's 'World in Action' led to him first joining the groundbreaking Glasgow Media Group, pioneers in deconstructing the implicit, and sometimes explicit, biases of television news and then to writing perceptively about the nature of the documentary genre and the broader history of mass communications, producing a number of landmark books in both areas. But it was his last work, investigating the roots of fake news and the lying that goes with it, that I found of particular interest at this historical juncture. Brian's understanding of the evolution of fake news is helping us create new insights into the current state of political communications.

Ivor Gaber

It is through contributions such as this that Brian was able to contribute to current debates. We will all miss those – almost as much as we will miss his lively and engaging conversation, his wit and above all his friendship. The lasting memorial to Brian is his academic work and the memories that those of us who knew him are privileged to treasure.

Ivor Gaber is Professor of Political Journalism at the University of Sussex and a former radio and television producer and political correspondent for BBC TV and Radio, ITV, Channel Four and Sky News.

BOOK REVIEWS

The roots of fake news: Objecting to objective journalism
Brian Winston and Matthew Winston
London and New York, Routledge pp 211
ISBN: 9780367145453 (hbk);
9780367145460 (pbk); 9780429032264 (ebk)

Since the 2016 election of US President Donald Trump, a plethora of studies has been written on the topic of 'fake news'. Most of these works treat 'fake news' as a new phenomenon and focus on the role of social media as a distribution platform during the 2016 US election and other recent events like the Brexit referendum. Recent scholarship on 'fake news' has major limitations: studies tend to focus on a narrow range of communication activities and hardly interrogate the role which 'fake news' historically played in Anglophone societies. There is also a lack in scholarship that assesses 'fake news' in the context of the cultural and ideological practices of liberal journalism. Brian Winston and Matthew Winston rectify these shortfalls in their very impressive media history on the roots of 'fake news'.

The father and son duo identify a current 'fake news panic' of an 'ahistorical, ungrounded and hysterical' nature on the one hand while on the other hand arguing that this episode shines light 'on legitimate journalism's inevitable shortcomings' that long needed to be addressed (p. 103). According to Winston and Winston, 'fake news' is a centuries-old and not a new problem crucially linked to the practices of journalism. The news may be 'undermined by mendacities but is, far more often, comprised by accidental errors' or diluted 'by incompleteness and subjectivity', Winston and Winston argue (p. 13). They further suggest that such evident shortfalls of journalism may be exploited by various political actors because they are not sufficiently addressed by scholars and the profession.

There exists a 'fake news/news dichotomy', Winston and Winston further write, that 'serves to re-enforce a vision of good and bad media which comforts "good" (all too often simply meaning "mainstream") media' (p. 12). Moreover, this dichotomy enables 'Trumpian attacks' on the media 'because journalism promises what it conspicuously fails to deliver' (pp 12-13). Hence, Winston and Winston see the main problem 'located in the ideology and practice of journalism itself' arguing that 'the more loudly it insists on its truth, the greater its threat to its credibility' (pp 12-13). Hence, to counter the problem of 'fake news' requires a reconsideration of the functions and normative standards as well as the expectations that society ascribes to the journalistic profession.

The authors make a well-evidenced historically and theoretically based case for their argument. The foreword sets 'fake news' in the context of objective journalism. After that, the first part unpacks the history of news to assess the 'roots' of the issue. Winston and Winston argue that the 'fake news' phenomenon is 'not just older than Facebook et al, it is older than the newspaper itself, or the presses used to print it' (p. 17). Starting in 1485, the book unravels the relationship between news and truth (or untruths i.e., 'fake news') covering various periods from the development of the printing press to newspapers, news media, legacy media, digital news and news platforms. The second part of the book delivers the context of the study by way of assessing the notions of 'objectivity' and 'truth' from various perspectives including science, law and moral philosophy. Winston and Winston conclude that the news should not make unattainable truth claims:

> The bottom line remains: journalists eschew the protocols of science, 'hard' or 'soft', attainable or otherwise. The accuracy of the representations their protocols produce are of a different order. Claiming honoured professional status in the face of such difference is to distract from the crucial functions of the press, which can be exercised without this accolade. Making such a claim is to open a can of worms and be eaten by them – a situation arguably in progress, with the 'fake news' attacks. Claiming any consanguinity with the sciences, like other claims to various flavours of objectivity, is, as we have been arguing, to give a hostage to fortune (p. 129).

The final two chapters nicely pull together the elements discussed in the first two sections looking at the role of the contemporary fourth estate. Winston and Winston end with their 'idea of an honest, subjective, biased foundation on which journalism may be rebuilt' (p. 199). For that to be fulfilled, they suggest a return to Michael Schudson's six core functions of journalism: to provide information about what is not generally known, to investigate as guardians those who should be the guardians of public welfare, to be a public forum for the expression of ideas and opinions, to analyse the context in which events occur, to encourage 'social empathy' better to understand 'how the other half lives' and to mobilise, in the name of partisanship, like-minded groups of the citizenry (pp 199-200).

According to Winston and Winston, institutionalising these arrays would result in the news addressing the audience as a 'political body', thereby acknowledging 'that different groups have different opinions' rather than the current idea which fosters the understanding that one side is 'objectively right' (p. 200). Such a change away from the 'myth of objective journalism', they finally propose, would disable 'the worst mainstream-media offenders, when it comes to faking, twisting, distorting the news' (p. 200).

Winston and Winston have produced a formidable study on the roots of the 'fake news' crisis and how it could be mitigated. The book is a must read for scholars, students and journalists interested in understanding how the intricate relationship between journalism, truth and 'fake news' has built up over centuries.

**Florian Zollmann,
Senior Lecturer in Journalism,
Newcastle University, UK**

It's the media, stupid! Essays in honour of Brian Winston

Richard Lance Keeble (ed.)

Bury St Edmunds, Abramis Publishing, 2022 pp 198

ISBN: 9781845497965

It's the media, stupid! is an entirely non-stupid discussion of important issues arising from our ever-changing media landscape. The essays are intelligent and stimulating, collected together expertly by editor Richard Lance Keeble in honour of Brian Winston's remarkable career as journalist, seminal scholar, historian of media, advocate of free media and witty, courageous provocateur of sometimes unfashionable ideas.

There is historical continuity amid the ten chapters: some of the main issues have been around for a long time: freedom of expression, media harm and the perennial debate on objectivity. There is also novelty: the social and media contexts in which the issues occur have changed, and the chapters reflect this evolution.

Media scholarship and media ethics are now practised in a chaotic world of global media where ethical issues have burst through the walls of professional newsrooms to include citizen journalism, new forms of engaged journalism and online extreme speech by racists, demagogues, hackers and trolls. The latter engage in communication violence. There is a global misinformation war – deliberate, malicious and financed by states and other political forces. The toxicity of public channels of communication has, then, become a major ethical, legal, and cultural problem in a plural and interconnected world.

Keeble does an admirable job of summarising the chapters' contents in his helpful introduction. Also, two appendixes provide background on Winston's stellar career, including an interview with Winston. I focus on three major issues that run throughout the book and give the manuscript a thematic unity. Like the chapter authors, I come to praise Winston. Yet I also speak freely where I have reservations or questions. I think Winston would approve of that approach.

The book's three common themes are at the heart of Winston's scholarship: freedom of expression and media publication, the value (or lack of value) of journalism objectivity and how to respond to irresponsible media content that causes serious harm. The issues are connected. How should freedom of publication be legitimately restrained by law or other mechanisms where the publications are false, racist or intolerant? Would our media system work better if journalists abandoned their traditional dogma about objectivity as a neutral reporting of 'just the facts'?

The notion of objectivity is scarcely separable from notions of truth and what is real. Thus, the first of three sections in the book contains four chapters that deal with 'claiming the real' through documentaries. The first two chapters by Tom Waugh and Deane Williams, respectively, call attention to the work of Canadian Magnus Isacsson and German critical film theorist Siegfried Kracauer (1889-1966). In 'The documentaries of Magnus Isacsson (1948-2012): A case study in the local and the global', Waugh argues persuasively that Isacsson is too little recognised as a great documentary maker. He notes Isacsson's 'non-objective' method of giving voice to marginal or non-conforming heroic individuals in Canada – French, English and Aboriginal. It shows the power of focusing on 'subjectivity'. Williams, in 'Naïve realism: Repositioning Kracauer's theory', reflects on Kracauer's theoretical writings to offer a 'redemption' of the term 'naïve realism' in the history of film, photography and the arts generally. Naïve realism captures people, places and events in ways that are uncontrived, spontaneous, authentic and not burdened with theoretical sophistication. The artist also attempts to work in a spontaneous manner. Thus, we get objective bits of what is real, not 'staged' reality, one achieves an 'objective naïvete'. Unlike mimesis – copying an object according to conventional rules – Kracauer sees photography and other good artworks as 'rendering nature as it exists independently of us'. Williams notes how this seeking of the naïve is similar to the idea that philosophy should recapture lived experience or the 'lifeworld', as in the writings of phenomenologist Edmund Husserl. There is also some similarity with the surrealist's avant-garde aim to create art spontaneously from subconscious impulses.

Kate Nash, with 'Covid-19 conspiracy documentary: Claiming the real in a context of uncertainty', and Annette Hill, with 'The act of watching documentary', round out the section. Nash considers the techniques and strategies used by Covid-19 conspiracy documentaries to create pandemic counter-narratives. Rather than dismiss such work as simply false, Nash shows how the films 'claim the real' by using some of the methods of non-conspiratorial works, such as citing alleged experts and using scientific facts and theories where convenient. This gives the documentaries an 'epistemic authority' for viewers already cynical about institutions, officials and mainstream media. Meanwhile, Hill urges scholars to study more carefully 'the art of watching documentary' – the 'complex engagement of audiences' as they reflect on the meaning and value of such works.

Waugh and Williams show how notions of what is real and objective can be conceived in different ways and how media work is enriched by a diversity of approaches. Williams provides insight into artistic naïve realism but whether one is impressed by this approach, and wants to rehabilitate it, depends largely on one's epistemology and aesthetic philosophy. Philosophers, some time ago, abandoned naïve realism as a way to think about empirical knowledge. They talked about the 'myth of the given' in experience. There was no spontaneous, unmediated contact with reality – usually regarded as direct sensations. Even our sensations are grouped into *gestalts* which we interpret. The idea that one can render 'things in themselves' is a questionable notion inherited from Kant's idea of a noumenal world. Kant also initiated the seminal notion that all of our experience of reality is mediated. For Kant, the mediation consisted of an (innate) conceptual scheme that organises sensory intuitions. In art history, Ernst Gombrich (2002 [1960]) made a similar point almost two centuries after Kant: there is no 'innocent eye'.[1] Also, I am not sure that the surrealists were the naïve realists of the avant-garde. Their 'spontaneity' was a studied spontaneity, encumbered by theoretical notions about Freudian processes, hyper-reality and so on. Even the lived world of Husserl and Maurice Merleau-Ponty, although experiential and pre-scientific, is not a naïve realism about the world.

Section 2, 'Free expression, offence and critical human rights', begins with the most philosophically sophisticated chapter by American ethicist Clifford G. Christians, titled 'Humans as cultural beings in theory and practice'. In retrospect, this chapter may have been placed at the start of the book. It provides a systematic philosophical perspective on communication, communications ethics and how humans are, by necessity, interpreters. Humans create culture by communicating and interacting through symbols. I return later to this chapter.

The other two chapters of Section 2 deal with free speech amid harmful online publications. How to restrain clear and harmful abuses of the freedom to publish without censoring legitimate, critical expressions of opinion?

Julian Petley, in 'Doing harm: How the UK government threatens to impose online censorship', writes an informative critique of Britain's progress toward its first law against harmful online media. Petley warns that the online law 'threatens to impose online censorship' by countenancing messages that are offensive to people as worthy of legal restraint. Given the subjectivity of psychological reactions to media content, this move would seriously threaten legal speech which does not cause palatable harm to anyone. Starting from John Stuart Mill's famous 'harm principle' in *On liberty*, Petley argues for an online law based on real, significant and perceptual harm, such as when cyberbullying leads someone towards suicide, or online attacks on racial minorities create a climate of fear. Moreover, rather than one omnibus online law, Petley likes the idea of a number of focused laws about specific types of online media harm. He also approves of Winston's argument that the laws of online restraint should be dealt with by the courts, not government or bureaucratic structures. These strike me as sensible positions in the attempt to balance freedom and harm.

However, there is a voice of scepticism about one of Winston's ideas in the next chapter by Raphael Cohen-Almagor, in 'The price of ridiculing the prophet: The *Charlie Hebdo* affair'. He analyses the terror attack on the *Charlie Hebdo* offices, in Paris, on 7 January 2015. He argues that, in a plural world, where not everyone is a liberal, publishers who intend to publish controversial content have a responsibility to consider seriously the possible consequences of doing so – violent protests, increased tension among groups and attacks on journalists. They should be aware that freedom of speech 'has a price'. Further, Cohen-Almagor questions Winston's contention that in democratic societies, freedom of expression can only exist if there is also 'a right to offend' or ridicule. Cohen-Almagor is sceptical about any such right. Instead, he thinks there is a right to discuss and debate openly and frankly our different views on major and sensitive topics, while being respectful of other people. This is solid ethical advice for plural democracies seeking common ground and peaceful co-existence. However, it does not eliminate the problem of what to do with online voices that do not wish to abide by such norms.

The book concludes with Section 3, 'Objections to objectivity: Politics and ethics of the media'. Ivor Gaber, in 'Fake news, double spin and strategic lying in the post-truth era', contributes a thoughtful exposition of fake news as 'double spin' and 'strategic lying'. Martin Conboy, in 'The media of the past determining the politics of the future?' dissects the coverage of British national daily newspapers on the Brexit vote on 31 January 2020. Conboy concludes that many of the images and messages were an expression of the conservative values of older generations for whom strong nationalism is still meaningful, but less meaningful to younger generations. The book concludes on a constructive note. Pratāp Rughani writes an inspiring piece on how to practise a journalism that brings rival groups together, rather than create divisions, by adopting practices of restorative justice pioneered in countries such as South Africa.

Objectivity redoux
I conclude by discussing how objectivity in journalism is understood and criticised in this book. It haunts many of the chapters. This gives me an opportunity to suggest an alternate way of understanding the concept. I also note how media studies and media ethics, in particular, need to become more advocational and global.

I have spent much of my career writing about the history of objectivity in Western culture, not just in the history of journalism. I also have proposed an alternate conception of objectivity that I call 'pragmatic objectivity' which is situated and embedded in history, and attempts to meet valid criticisms of the original or 'traditional' notion of news objectivity. In *The invention of journalism ethics: The path to objectivity and beyond* (2015 [2005]), I examined how news objectivity was only one conception of objectivity and was based on an outdated epistemology derived mainly from 19th century positivism with its many dualisms of fact and value, observation and interpretation, and reason and emotion. I discussed how objectivity has taken many forms going back to the origins of rational philosophy in Greek antiquity. For instance, there is ontological objectivity where a belief 'fits' or is 'true to the object' or the world; an epistemological objectivity which emphasises the testing of belief. Epistemic objectivity is the testing of beliefs and published material for evidence, facts and logic, given the best available criteria of cognitive evaluation. There is also moral objectivity which asks humans, in various contexts, to make public decisions using objective and fair criteria, such as when hiring a new professor or when a jury considers a verdict.

Objectivity in Western journalism, as an explicit doctrine, only arose in the early 20th century after centuries of partisan and opinion journalism. However, in the second half of the 19th century, objective reporting was anticipated by an interest in factual news reports for the emerging mass commercial newspapers, which sought a wide readership. The newspapers (and professional journalism societies) introduced strict rules about reporting just the facts, balancing voices, being neutral and not expressing one's opinion. Why this was thought to be necessary I won't go into, but one justification was to reduce partisan bias and persuade a sceptical public that the news could be trusted. This method of writing and editing news reports became popular, especially in North American mainstream news media and among public broadcasters more globally. The first explicit North American codes of journalism in the early 1900s praised objectivity as the sign of a professional commitment to the public interest. During the heyday of objectivity – circa 1920 to 1970 – the doctrine came under increasing attack from journalists, academics and social groups, such as anti-war and civil rights activists. Positivism died, thankfully; and a more perspectival and engaged journalism returned, especially on the internet. Still, the values of traditional news objectivity persist. When Donald Trump became president, many American news organisations tied themselves in knots trying to be 'objective' while wondering whether they should report that the president was a bald-faced liar or a racist with a fondness for anti-black extreme organisations. Even if true, was it not a violation of neutrality for reporters to make these assertions? What was needed was an alternate conception of a non-neutral objectivity that allowed for engagement and the drawing of well-evidenced conclusions – not the abandonment of the idea of objectivity *per se*.

Pragmatic objectivity holds that epistemic objectivity is the central, valid notion in all of this debate. Objectivity is not about repressing feeling or passion, not about neutrality, not about reporting just the facts. In an era when facts are manufactured, a passive stenography of fact is ripe for manipulation. In an era when democracy is under attack, society needs journalism that is engaged in its defence. Pragmatic objectivity is about being willing to test one's journalism, one's opinions, one's sentiments and one's biases by a holistic array of criteria of evaluation that go beyond an appeal to isolated facts. It includes logical consistency, clarity of concept, support from existing forms of knowledge, ability to withstand public scrutiny, an openness to learn from other perspectives, altering one's beliefs in the face of counter evidence, and so on. None of this will give you absolute, unsituated knowledge but that is not the purpose of inquiry or journalism. The aim is to secure the best fallible knowledge possible.

We seek well-evidenced beliefs and explanations which get us closer to some set of truths about some phenomenon – given our situation, the available methods and what we now know. What pragmatic objectivity gives us is a consistent framework from which to do evidence-based journalism within our situated lives. It is an imperfect, all-too-human approach. It is a flexible stance that can apply to many forms of journalism – not just straight news reporting. Great journalism, in my view, is a convergence of passion and testing, subjectivity and objectivity. Passion alone tends toward ranting, bias, conspiracy theory or fake news. Traditional objectivity alone often results in mincing neutrality and a perpetuation of the status quo. Journalists need a passion for, and a courage to do, significant, deep stories that are also tested for evidence, facts and logic. This is what it means to be rational and reasonable. As I wrote in *Objectively engaged journalism* (2019), we need an epistemology of practice grounded in an 'objectivity with a human face' or an 'objectivity *in situ*'.

It is from this perspective that I view the references to objectivity in this book. On the disappointing side, I find that some authors simply presume that objectivity is as dubious notion. It is as if 'subjectivity' has a halo around it while 'objectivity' has a dark rain cloud above it. Some authors also appear to assume that objectivity in journalism is (or must be) synonymous with the outdated creed of traditional objectivity. But society has moved on. In science alone, notions of objectivity are neither positivistic nor reductionistic but holistic, incorporating imagination and passion. One can derive a scientific hypothesis from whatever source you wish – emotion, imagination or dreams. But you will then be asked to seek confirming or disconfirming evidence through hopefully rigorous methods. Science is not a monolithic creature, it is *not* cold and 'just the facts' objectivity. It is not the enemy of the humanities, of passion or even subjectivity. Today, some of the deepest work on the mind, on emotion and on subjective experience is to be found not only in the humanities or in art, but also in evolutionary psychology, social psychology, the social sciences and the extension of the brain sciences to such areas as aesthetic and moral experience. However, science – and all rational inquiry – is the enemy of unjustified assertion, reckless opinion and the irresponsible use of the freedom to publish.

In the book, I don't see many authors presenting a clear alternative to objectivity. If we abandon objectivity, what other norms will fill the normative vacuum? It is not enough to wave one's hands and say something vague about expressing or investigating subjectivity. We need to be both specific and systematic in fashioning a different normative framework. We can deconstruct our concepts of truth, objectivity and rationality but we should not stop there. We need to *reconstruct* these notions for our era. Otherwise, we simply perpetuate the unproductive dualistic debate between subjectivists and objectivists.

This is why I admire Christians's philosophy of the human, with its emphasis on pluralism, holism, and truth – all at the same time. Christians sees interpretation as situated in history and empowered by culturally derived symbolic systems. Yet, like me, he thinks we can still talk intelligibly about better or worse interpretations and about 'interpretive sufficiency', given our frameworks of thought – frameworks that evolve and change. I regard inquiry (and philosophy) as immanent thinking. We do not think from a place outside the world or outside of history. As Merleau-Ponty wrote: philosophy, the act of 'seeing things anew', is 'itself within history, it too draws upon the world and upon constituted reason'.[2]

I agree with Winston that what I call traditional objectivity is a dubious doctrine. But I wonder whether it is the most important problem for media today. *Redefining* objectivity strikes me as a major challenge. Also, one could just as easily argue that it is rampant subjectivity and irresponsible use of media freedom that is the main problem. Whatever the answer, there is no going back to the past and positivistic objectivity. Instead, we should welcome new and creative ways of telling stories that reveal the humanness and the subjective life of diverse groups of people. I only ask that such work be willing to subject itself to the test of what is rational; what is based on evidence; what is open, tolerant, and respectful in attitude and what survives honest (not contrived) intersubjective scrutiny. For too long, too many academics have indulged in a fashionable scepticism about notions of rationality, truth and objectivity. We now have the phrase 'a post-truth era'. It fills me with fear for the future. I recall where that attitude has taken mankind in the past: murderous crusades, irrational love of tyrants, fascism and holocaust.

Publics *can* go irrational, like today. Media scholars and practitioners better be up to the task of opposing the undemocratic, irrational media that create such publics. This means that our conception of media ethics should be broadened beyond the academic study of media norms and practices. In a world where democracy is in doubt and intolerance is rising, media ethics needs to be also a form of advocacy and engagement, and it needs to become a global media ethics where norms are grounded in humanitarian principles.[3] Ethicists, media scholars, journalism schools, centres for democracy and NGOs who care about good media need to form coalitions for 'macro-resistance' – a society-wide (or globally) coordinated effort to detox the public channels of information through public-inclusive initiatives, web sites and media ethics education. We need to create tolerant media spaces where citizens are informed by a journalism that is both democratically engaged and pragmatically objective.

The future of humane society and egalitarian democracy depends on the maintenance of reasonable, reality-based publics in the face of conspiratorial, unreasonable publics and extreme political parties. *That* requires action, not only analysis.

Notes
[1] Gombrich, *The Art of Illusion*

[2] Merleau-Ponty, *The Phenomenology of Perception*, pp 84-85

[3] For writings on global media ethics, see my recent *Handbook of Global Media Ethics*

References
Gombrich, Ernst (2002 [1960]) *Art and illusion: A study in the psychology of pictorial representation*, London, Phaidon

Merleau-Ponty, Maurice (2014 [1945]) *The phenomenology of perception*, trans. by Landes, Donald A., New York, Routledge

Ward, Stephen J. A. (2015 [2005]) *The invention of journalism ethics: The path to objectivity and beyond*, Montreal, McGill-Queen's University

Ward, Stephen J. A. (2019) *Objectively engaged journalism: An ethic*, Montreal, McGill-Queen's University Press

Ward, Stephen J. A. (ed.) (2021) *Handbook of global media ethics*. Cham, Springer Nature

Dr Stephen J. A. Ward is an ethicist, historian of ideas and professor emeritus of the University of British Columbia, Canada. He has authored and edited 10 books on ethics, media ethics and the history of ideas.

PAPER

Nanna Vedel-Hertz
Allaina Kilby

The sound of silence: European news coverage of refugees in Greece and what is left unreported

When covering migration and its challenges, the news media often turn to politicians as trusted and reliable sources while rarely representing refugee voices. These sourcing habits create what we call 'areas of silence', which mean that the public is not presented with satisfactory nor accurate coverage of refugees. This research explored how these areas of silence are produced. It analysed 395 articles from France, UK and Germany to establish the overall patterns of reporting. These findings reinforce existing research examining the representation of refugees. The research also reports on nine qualitative interviews conducted with volunteers and refugees on the Greek island of Lesvos that offer a powerful alternative perspective to academic and news representations of refugees. The research highlights a need for journalists to utilise a broader range of sources and to challenge the current discourse in their reporting of refugees in Greece.

Keywords: primary definers, refugee crisis, watchdog, Greece, representation

Introduction

When becoming a refugee, one also loses the natural rights of citizenship (Arendt 1967; Agamben 1998; Nyers 2006), so having access to arenas where one's voice can be heard is paramount. Since the normative purpose of the news media is to foster an open discussion and hold people in power to account (Manning 2001; Thorbjørnsrud and Figenshou 2014) it could serve as a platform for refugee voices. Yet, silencing refugees has become a taken-for-granted routine accomplishment in European news (Chouliaraki and Zabarowski 2017). As this research shows, it is a routine that excludes important knowledge and nuances about the plight and experiences of refugees.

The number of forcibly displaced people is growing and by the end of 2020 the UNHCR estimated that there were more than 82.4 million forcibly displaced people worldwide (UNHCR 2021). As Figure 1 shows, 48 million are internally displaced, 20.7 million are refugees and 4.1 million are asylum-seekers (ibid). There is, thus, a greater need than ever for an arena where forcibly displaced people can have their voices heard and portrayed accurately.

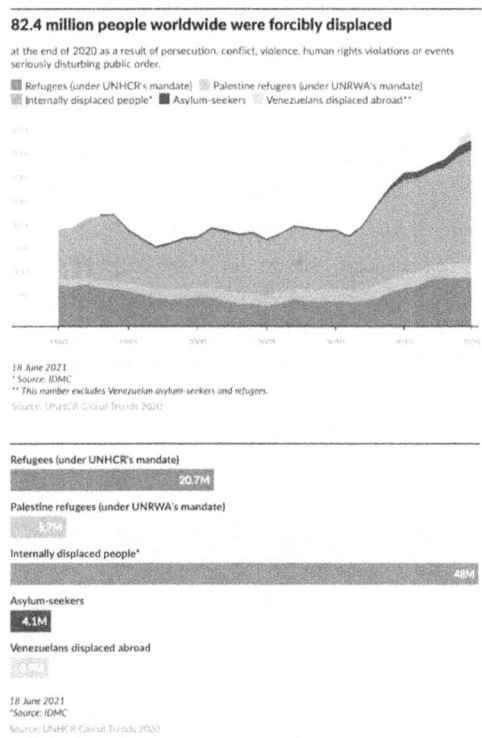

Figure 1. UNHRC statistics on forcibly displaced people worldwide

When the so-called 'refugee crisis' in Europe started in 2015, there was a sentiment in the news media that refugees coming to Europe should be helped and were welcome (Chouliaraki and Zabarowski 2017; Gray and Franck 2019). However, during November and December 2015 the media discourse shifted to border security and refugees became portrayed much more as a threat to Europe. Further changes in coverage were precipitated by the November terrorist attacks in Paris and the New Year's Day attacks in Germany (Chouliaraki and Zabarowski 2017; Gray and Franck 2019). Gray and Franck (2019) show that the events were not directly related to refugees, yet were linked from the initial reports in media and comments by politicians. As a result, they found, reporting of refugee voices decreased.

**Nanna
Vedel-Hertz
Allaina Kilby**

Since 2015, both media coverage of refugees coming to Europe and scholarly research have decreased, yet refugee numbers continue to increase, particularly in countries such as Greece, Spain and Italy (UNHCR 2020b). Consequently, there is still a need to investigate the news coverage of the situation in terms of the normative purpose of news. The question of whether refugees' own perspectives are routinely excluded is of particular importance. This paper firstly seeks to fill the research gap by investigating the current French, British and German coverage of refugees in Greece. It then goes a step further than previous research by examining what changes are needed in journalistic routines to break down the silence over refugee coverage. The paper reviews previous research, describes the methodological approach and then presents findings of the content analysis followed by the new insights that emerge from the interview data.

The importance of being heard

In democracies, the media is expected to maintain a free flow of ideas, foster open debate, allow a diverse range of sources to speak and hold people in power to account (see Manning 2001; Zelizer 2004; Boudana 2011). Objectivity remains a norm in much journalism and, in their search for this, journalists often turn to trusted sources (primary definers), allowing claims to objectivity to be maintained (Hall et al. 1978). The media, furthermore, plays a vital role in assigning meaning to events, debates and groups, making them more understandable for the general public (see Hall 2007 [1973]); Bailey and Harindranath 2005; Bødker 2014). In doing so they risk unconsciously drawing on taken-for-granted consensual viewpoints and cultural maps of the world and relying on primary definers (Hall et al. 1978; Bødker, 2014). Hence, being a primary definer (often politicians, governments and experts) enables such individuals to play a shaping role in the news (see Berkowitz 2008; Carlson and Franklin 2011; Bødker 2014). The creation of 'news' is, thus, a complex and often subconscious process, where an event is not simply and transparently reported, but made comprehensible for the audience through identifying it and assigning it to a social context (ibid). This process ultimately creates a 'primary interpretation' which 'then "commands the field" in all subsequent treatment and sets the terms of reference within which all further coverage or debate takes place' (Hall et al. 1978; 58). Under these conditions, when a primary interpretation is in place and commands the field, areas of silence are created, in which alternative perspectives and voices that do not fit the terms of reference are situated (Hall et al. 1978). It is important to note that these processes are regarded as ideological, that is, not a result of malevolent or conscious acts by media practitioners but rather the result of an unconscious reproduction of ideological assumptions about the world and the power relations inherent in it (ibid).

Processes that produce elite voices as primary definers and relegate others to areas of silence have been identified in the reporting of refugees and migration. A tendency to exclude refugee voices while relying heavily on politicians and government sources, who become primary definers, is well described (e.g. van Dijk 2000; Chouliaraki and Zaborowski 2017; Santos et al. 2018). In the media, refugees are often reduced to either victims or threats, ahistorical beings, the 'other' and part of a mass (Malkki 1996; Zetter 2007; Chouliaraki and Stolic 2019). The primary interpretation in European media leads to representations of refugees as a 'threat to national security', with the stress placed on the importance of border security (Chouliaraki and Zabarowski 2017; Gray and Franck 2019). Refugees are cast as the dangerous backwards 'other' who will ruin Europe if they settle there (Chouliaraki and Zabarowski 2017). This primary interpretation has its roots in the orientalist and heavily criticised thesis of a 'clash of civilisations', which predicts that the main source of future conflicts will be clashes between cultural and religious identities, most notably between the West and Islam (Huntington 1993, 1996; Allen 2010). The primary interpretation of border security was established during the 'refugee crisis' in 2015, the terror attacks in Paris and the sexual attacks in Germany (Chouliaraki and Zabarowski 2017; Gray and Franck 2019). Yet, once again, it is important to note that these studies do suggest that the primary interpretation became dominant not because of conscious actions, but because these ideological assumptions and power relations are so embedded in society, 'so common, so natural, so taken for granted' (Hall et al. 1978: 65) that they are hardly visible unless one purposefully sets out to expose them. Therefore, this research does not argue that journalists set out to reproduce problematic representations grounded in the discourses of threat to security, a backwards 'other' or a clash of civilizations, but instead critiques journalism's routine reliance on certain sources and socially available representations.

The silencing of refugees is a thoroughly researched topic (see Van Dijk 2000; Chouliaraki and Zaborowski 2017; Santos et al. 2018) but there is an absence of research investigating the perspectives and nuances possible if their voices were instead routinely included in news coverage. This research helps fill the knowledge deficit by interviewing nine sources who belong to groups normally excluded from mainstream news coverage. It will ask what is situated in the areas of silence that are created by the taken-for-granted, unconscious assumptions and power structures reproduced in the current media coverage. Most studies focus on analysing media coverage at the height of the 'refugee crisis' in 2015-16 underlining the sense that the crisis is over or has not changed since. Because that is not the case, the research here, that updates and explores the topic further, is of value.

Methodology
This research set out to expose the normalised, taken-for-granted, ideological constructs in media representations proposed in primary interpretation theory. The paper explores what is not reported and which questions are omitted, because of the established patterns. Two research questions were developed.

1. To what extent does the theory of 'primary definers' explain the news media's coverage of refugees in Greece?
2. What is left out of the news media's coverage of refugees in Greece?

To answer these questions, an explanatory sequential design is adopted (Ivankova et al. 2006). The initial quantitative content analysis of 395 articles leads to the line of questions applied in the nine qualitative interviews that follow.

Content analysis
We selected a sample of 395 articles via NexisUK from Germany, France and the UK because these are the countries that accept most asylum applications in Europe (European Parliament 2020). From Germany we selected one news agency, DPA International, and one newspaper, *Die Welt*. From France we selected one news agency, Agence France Presse. From the UK we selected two newspapers, *The Times* and *The Guardian*. English news was chosen as the common language because it made them accessible to refugees not fluent in either French or German. There was no press agency available using these search terms on NexisUK from the UK, so two newspapers were included instead to provide a more balanced sample.

The search terms were Greece, refugee, migrant, asylum seeker and immigrant. The timeframe was 1 September 2019 to 13 March 2020, since arrivals through the Aegean Sea increased from September 2019 (Aegean Boat Report 2020) until March 2020 when the spread of Covid-19 led to world-wide border closures. The variables to be coded were developed from the theoretical framework and focused on four overall themes:

1: general information (news outlet, country, length of article);
2: primary definers (e.g. number of sources and the category they belong to);
3: primary interpretation (e.g. did the reporting victimise refugees, highlight the importance of 'securing borders' and use water metaphors?);
4: coverage of refugees (e.g. does it mention solutions and speak of the 'refugee crisis'?).

Codes for positive reporting strategies (e.g. initiatives that could help refugees) were also developed, but were not found within the news sample.

Semi-structured interviews
The interviews enabled us to explore the areas of silence created by the primary interpretation and what was situated there. The interview sample included refugees and smaller NGOs and was based on a sampling mainly through the Facebook groups 'Information point for Lesvos volunteers' and 'Information point for Greek Volunteers'. Snowballing was also utilised. The interview guide was developed on the basis of findings from the content analysis and from existing literature on refugee coverage. Afterwards, a thematic analysis was carried out, developing initial data-driven codes based on points identified in the interview data.

Content analysis findings: 'They do not belong here'
The findings confirmed previous research in which refugees were depicted using water metaphors (van Dijk, 2000) in 62.5 per cent of the articles, as a threat (78.5 per cent), spoken of as overwhelming or uncontrollable (89.9 per cent). In addition, refugees were rarely used as sources. Overall, the patterns across the three countries were uniform, which suggests that there is a routinised neglect of refugee perspectives across European news. Figure 2 reveals that politicians were sourced in 87.1 per cent of the articles, making them the most primary of primary definers. The sources cited the most

after politicians were people associated with the EU (in 39 per cent of articles), followed by people associated with the UN (33.2 per cent) and NGOs or special interest groups (32.9 per cent). While NGOs and interest groups were present in the news, they were always reported secondarily and thus within the already defined primary interpretation.

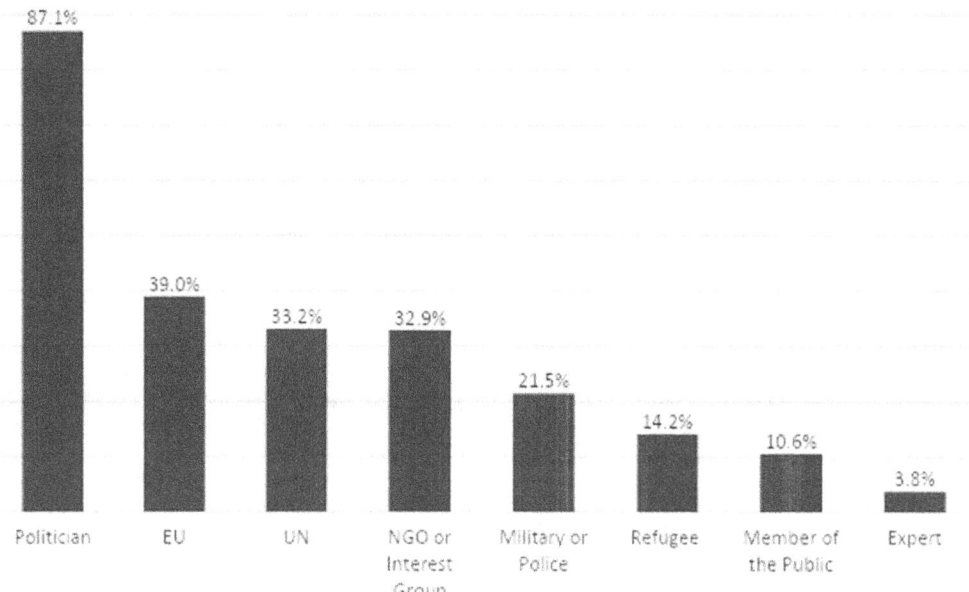

Figure 2. News sources

As found in previous studies (e.g. van Dijk 2000; Chouliaraki and Zaborowski 2017; Santos et al. 2018), refugees were less frequently cited – in this study, in 14.2 per cent of the articles. Members of the public were cited in 10.6 per cent and experts in only 3.8 per cent. For a source to be coded as an expert, the article had to categorise them explicitly as experts or researchers e.g. 'professor in international law' (Fennel, 2020). At this point journalists could draw on the primary interpretation of the 'refugee crisis' already created by primary definers, which may explain why experts were rarely used to make sense of the events.

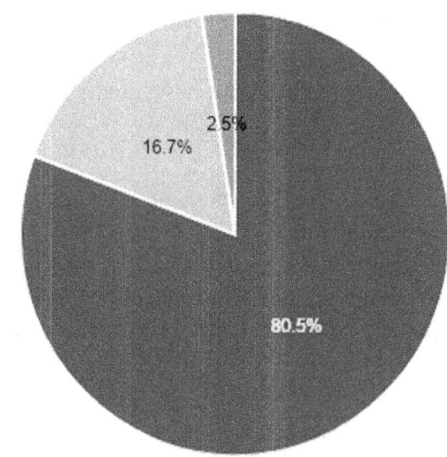

Figure 3. Border security as media focus

The primary interpretation focused on securing and protecting European borders against refugees. As Figure 3 shows, 80.5 per cent of the articles spoke of border security while, as can be seen in Figure 4, 84.2 per cent of the articles spoke of refugees solely in numbers. The primary interpretation thus appears to have barely changed since 2015, and seems to have dictated the future coverage of the topic (Hall et al. 1978). Additionally, as will become increasingly clear, there is almost no room left for other interpretations, further supporting the notion of areas of silence (Hall et al. 1978).

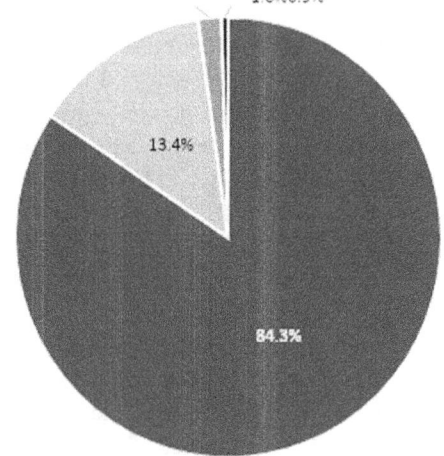

Figure 4. Refugees covered simply in term of statistics

Interview findings: Listening to the silence

To go a step further than previous studies, this research conducted nine interviews to investigate what might be situated in the areas of silence created by the primary interpretation and journalistic routines. The content analysis showed an over-use of politicians as sources. As a result, the refugees had little to no opportunity to mitigate their representations (see van Dijk 2000; Santos et al. 2018). To investigate the areas of silence three refugees, five volunteers and one journalist were interviewed. For their safety all interviewees have been given cover names:

Table 1. Interviewees

Name	Role
Amelia	NGO owner
Ella	Volunteer teacher
Benjamin	NGO owner
Olivia	Volunteer
Emma	Remote volunteer
John	Journalist
Sadia	Refugee, Volunteer
Aman	Refugee, Volunteer
Nabil	Refugee, Volunteer

The interviews suggest that, had volunteers and refugees been sourced more in mainstream media, the representation of refugees may have been mitigated. The interviewees did not describe refugees as helplessly sitting in the camps, as victims, nor as threats. All of the interviewees depicted refugees as actively seeking out ways to learn and secure a better future. Many of the NGOs also took on refugees as volunteers and all of the interviewed refugees either had or were still working for NGOs. NGO owner Benjamin said:

> That is the biggest misconception that the refugees have nothing to offer, that they are just a drain on the society. It is actually the reverse (Benjamin).

While the interviewees also spoke of refugees in terms of numbers, the refugees were simultaneously humanised by explaining their hopes and their motivations – depicting refugees not as people to fear, but who could be beneficial to the host country, For example:

> They are amazing because they are taking matters into their own hands and trying with the little that they have to make something for themselves (Emma).

> I pay taxes like a normal Greek (Aman).

Although the media did mention that conditions for the refugees in the Greek camps were bad, the reports rarely went into detail. In the interviews, this was a prevalent theme: island overcrowding, hour-long lines for everything from food and toilet facilities to asylum services. This was especially the case in the Moria camp, on the island of Lesvos, which the interviewees described as extremely dirty and unsanitary:

> I was so shocked to see the degradation and the unbelievably dire conditions. ... 20,000 people just left to fester (Ella).

> You know I have seen way too many suicides. Way too many people just cease to function from the trauma of Moria (Amelia, referring to a fire which destroyed a refugee camp in Moria in September 2020).

The changes that have happened on Lesvos since the initial stages of the 'refugee crisis' in 2015-2016 were also highlighted in the interviews:

> In 2015 people had hope. They would leave. Today, I still have people here from 2016 who are working through their asylum process (Amelia).

> It is really quite different because they don't care. ... if you are a minor you stay in the camp or in a tent... if a woman is pregnant or if you have special needs there is no difference now (Nabil).

The findings from the content analysis suggest that the primary interpretation established since the 'refugee crisis' had not developed much since. However, had the news media sought out the views of people on the ground important perspectives about the current situation on Lesvos could have been explained to the public. Hence, the accuracy of the current reporting is put at risk by reproducing the primary interpretation of border security. Many interviewees demanded that media hold people in power accountable for the current conditions. For instance, the journalist commented:

> Confront the politicians with what is going on, and to investigate what kind of money is being used. That is something that is truly lacking (John).

Again, it is important to note that while it can seem intentional that journalists reproduce the primary interpretation and rely on politicians as primary definers, this is not assumed here. The journalistic pursuit of objectivity and the internal pressures of news production likely create these patterns, which become so inherent that neither journalists nor editors are aware of them (Hall et al. 1978). Hence, these findings show a general need to investigate the journalistic routines to help identify which sources are naturally seen as objective and which are not.

'What I see is not migration, I see desperation'

Another theme of the interviewee talk was that refugees' human right to apply for asylum was being violated since they could not come to Europe legally.

> Europe's policy encourages people to come illegally, there is no legal way to apply for a five-year visa to come work in the EU (Amelia).

Consequently, the primary interpretation that focused on the refugees and their actions as illegal was rejected through use of a human rights discourse about rights being violated. The interviewees, furthermore, seemed to agree that all the people on Lesvos were – at least to a large degree – refugees, and therefore had more rights than what were currently being recognised.

> It is rather the fragmentation of human beings and their worth, if you are really well-off you are a refugee. Refugees have a right to protection. If you are a migrant then you are not as well-off. It is people who do not really have the right to try to get a better life by travelling to another country (John).

> They are playing with language; there are ratified laws that state what a nation must do in response to refugees arriving on their shores. If you don't call them refugees you don't have to do any of those things (Benjamin).

The findings align with previous research arguing that categorising people via the legal, political and cultural labels of asylum seeker and economic immigrant moves the focus from helping refugees to safety and gaining/maintaining human rights and instead puts it on securing borders (Daniel, 2002; Zetter, 2007; Limbu, 2009). Several of the interviewees stated that war was not the only justifiable reason for fleeing. Thus, through the eyes of the interviewees, the refugees are seen as people whose very last chance of survival was to come to Europe; they were, indeed, not running towards Europe but from the situation in their home country. Overall, the interviewees entirely accepted refugees' escape to Europe, arguing that they had a right to refuge on the continent.

> We have a certain amount of responsibility for the past and the present of these countries. So if you are driven out of your home by environmental issues or ... economic issues if you cannot survive then you are a refugee (Amelia).

The view that all people on Lesvos deserve to come to Europe is in stark contrast to the news coverage which, although speaking of refugees as victims, does not see them as having a right to come to Europe. The 1951 UN Convention says that a refugee is someone who 'owing to a well-founded fear of being persecuted for reasons of race, religion, nationality, membership of a particular group or political opinion has crossed an international border to seek protection' (Nyers 2006: 13).

The news media plays an important role of making meaning of events, especially those that the audience will not encounter directly (Goodman et al. 2017). Thus, when the news media report within a primary interpretation that sees most of the people coming to Greece as migrants, and therefore, as coming out of choice, this will be an important determinant in how the public understands the situation. Hence, when journalists rely unreflectively on their routines and previous interpretations, they do a disservice to the people on Lesvos who are being denied a basic human right.

These interpretations are difficult to dislodge. A primary interpretation constructing refugees coming to Greece as a matter of border security would force out the statements of volunteers and refugees, even if these speakers were included in the coverage. Counter-perspectives and points declaring a right to come are so far removed from the framework of border security as to be near-impossible to include in the coverage.

A bitter-sweet crack in the patterns

The situation regarding Covid-19 seemed to have given refugees a rare opportunity to be heard, as some were employed briefly to produce news items for, among others, the BBC and CNN. For a moment, it became evident that the reliance on a small number of primary definers was not inevitable. Benjamin reported that some of his students had media training, allowing them to be drawn on during the Covid-19 lockdown:

> Our students [refugees] are the only eyes and ears on the ground who are professionally trained and they are documenting everything and now it is the media that is coming to us. ... Well, it's a bitter sweet opportunity. It could not have come without a pandemic (Benjamin).

Emma, who volunteered for an NGO, monitoring the news coverage of the NGO and its sister organisation that focused on Covid-19, made a similar observation. Both NGOs were mostly made up of volunteer refugees on the ground and she observed that the situation gave the volunteer refugees a rare chance to be heard in the news media in relation to this specific event.

These examples suggest that when there are no other ways to secure the story, journalists will turn to refugees as sources. Thus, journalists can change their working routines if the situation calls for it, but it seems will do so only in extreme situations, because their news gathering routines are so embedded (Hall et al. 1978). Therefore, the changes that occurred during the Covid-19 pandemic are likely to fade, as they were a result of the circumstances, not operational changes in news production. Nonetheless, they show that it is possible.

A positive and humane perspective towards refugees emerges from the interviews, along with a richer description of the current situation in Greece. These perspectives were not present in the news media's coverage, confirming the extent to which current journalistic routines create areas of silence. These findings also show that new perspectives can emerge even when just a small step is taken outside current sourcing patterns, enriching the current debate. However, if the current primary interpretation is reproduced, the perspectives represented by the new sources might still be excluded from the coverage simply because they do not fit the overall primary interpretation of border security. Thus, a broader range of sources is not enough; journalists need to become aware of the taken-for-granted patterns, ideological assumptions and power relations they are unknowingly reproducing.

Discussion: Voice matters

While the purpose of this research was not to criticise the news media, the findings do show that European journalism falls short of its role when assigning meaning to refugees in Greece. It becomes clear that the current news coverage is so focused on furthering European self-interest that some perspectives and stories become stuck in the areas of silence created by journalistic routines. Since the patterns of reporting, and the areas of silence they create are a result of the inherent structures and routines in the news production, rather than conscious choices (Hall et al. 1978), this research strongly calls for a need to re-evaluate these structures and operational routines.

It also became clear that being included as a source does not matter in and of itself, if the primary interpretation (e.g. border security) is in place. Hence, along with changing their sourcing routines, journalists also need to question the taken-for-granted truths about the world and society that they unknowingly reproduce. If the patterns pointed out here are to change, refugee voices need to be included on equal terms with other definers of the issue. They, furthermore, need to be allowed to establish and mitigate the primary interpretation. Thus, what is needed is a questioning of the naturalness with which some sources' testimonies are cast as believable and objective and thus allowed to define our mediated reality, while others are not included due to journalistic routines. There is also a grave need for more sources, and a primary interpretation that allows for a more nuanced depiction of the situation, the refugees, and what it means for Europe if the news media is to live up to its normative role in democracy.

Conclusion: Only a small part of the truth

This research sought to go a step further than previous studies by exploring examples of what the media fails to report on when it comes to refugees in Greece, because of established journalistic routines and the areas of silence they create. There were clear patterns of the dominance of primary definers and a primary interpretation in the sample. The primary interpretation had seemingly become so dominant and narrowly focused on border security that other perspectives were excluded. Politicians were cast as primary definers and neither they

Nanna Vedel-Hertz
Allaina Kilby

nor their statements were challenged, which allowed them to maintain the primary interpretation of border security. The research also found that refugees were, to a large extent, othered and dehumanised. Consequently, the news coverage of refugees in Greece had gone mostly unchanged since the 'refugee crisis' in 2015-2016.

Taking just a small step outside of the media's current habits and interviewing nine sources on the island of Lesvos highlighted completely new perspectives and nuances. However, most of these perspectives did not directly contest the current primary interpretation of border security and there is therefore a risk that they would not be reported if the primary interpretation is not also changed. What this research argues is that the inclusion of a wider variety of sources is not enough, if they are not simultaneously allowed to question and challenge the current primary interpretation.

One of the authors as well as the interviewed journalist, John, both experienced how – even when journalists try to include refugee voices on equal terms with other primary definers – the piece is often not accepted, is edited to be within the primary interpretation or is cast as an alternative to news such as solutions journalism.

This research highlights how journalistic patterns of refugee coverage, established in 2015-2016, were still prevalent in 2019-20. Thus, the public were not provided with a satisfactory representation of the situation in Greece. It became clear that the primary interpretation of refugees had become so narrow that it created areas of silence. The primary interpretation of border security defined how journalists analysed, interpreted and understood the events. It seems that through the routines with which the journalists strive for objectivity they, unknowingly, disregard other normative standards such as impartiality and accuracy. However, this research has shown that there is room for changing these routines and that, in times of extreme circumstances, such as Covid-19, refugees can become trusted and reliable sources, as well as media producers themselves. Perhaps now is the time for news organisations to acknowledge that objectivity is not achieved by allowing normative primary definers to set the terms of representation, and that it is, in fact, strengthened by including the voices of people living through the situation first-hand.

Declaration of Conflicting Interests
The authors declare no potential conflicts of interest with respect to the research, authorship, and/or publication of this article. The authors received no financial support for the research, authorship, and/or publication of this article.

References

ABR (2020) Weekly reports, *Aegean Boat Report*. Available online at https://aegeanboatreport.com/weekly-reports/, accessed on 2 March 2020

Agamben, G. (1998) *Homo sacer: Sovereign power and bare life*, Stanford, CA, Stanford University Press

Allen, C. (2010) *Islamophobia*, Surrey, Ashgate Publishing Limited

Arendt, H. (1967) *The origins of totalitarianism*, New York, Harcourt, Brace and Company

Bailey, O. G. and Harindranath, R. (2005) Racialized 'othering': The representation of asylum seekers in news media, Allan, S. (ed.) *Journalism: Critical issues*, Berkshire: Open University Press pp 274-286

BBC (2015) Paris attacks: What happened on the night?, 9 December. Available online at https://www.bbc.com/news/world-europe-34818994, accessed on 2 February 2021

Boudana S. (2011) A definition of journalistic objectivity as a performance, *Media, Culture & Society*. Vol. 33, No. 3 pp 385-398

Bødker, H. (2014) Journalism as cultures of circulation, *Digital Journalism*, Vol. 3, No. 1 pp 101-115

Carlson, M. and Franklin, B. (2011) Introduction, Franklin, B. and Carlson, M. (eds), *Journalists, sources and credibility*, London and New York, Routledge pp 1-15

Chouliaraki, L. and Zaborowski, R. (2017) Voice and community in the 2015 refugee crisis: A content analysis of news coverage in eight European countries, *International Communication Gazette*, Vol. 70 pp 613-635

Chouliaraki, L. and Stolic, T. (2019) Photojournalism as political encounter: Western news photography in the 2015 migration 'crisis', *Visual Communication*, Vol. 13, No. 3 pp 311-331

Daniel, E. V. (2002) The refugee: A discourse on displacement, MacClancy, J. (ed.) *Exotic no more: Anthropology on the front lines*, Chicago, University of Chicago Press pp 270-286

European Parliament (2020) *A welcoming Europe?* Available online at https://www.europarl.europa.eu/infographic/welcoming-europe/index_en.html#filter=2018, May

Fennel, E. (2020) Border battles: Professor David Owen on refugees and international law: Law diary, *Times*, 12 March. Available online at https://www.thetimes.co.uk/article/border-battles-professor-david-owen-on-refugees-and-international-law-6k9vh57bm, accessed on 7 February 2022

Georgiou, M. (2017) Does the subaltern speak? Migrant voices in digital Europe, *Popular Communication*, Vol. 16, No. 1 pp 45-57

Goodman, S., Sirriyeh, A. and McMahon, S. (2017) The evolving (re)categorisations of refugees throughout the 'refugee/migrant crisis', *Journal of Community & Applied Social Psychology*, Vol. 27 pp 105-114

Gray, H. and Franck, A. (2019) Refugees as/at risk: The gendered and racialized underpinnings of securitization in British media narratives, *Security Dialogue*, Vol. 50, No. 3 pp 275-291

Hall, S. (2007) 1973]) Encoding and decoding in the television discourse, *CCCS selected working papers*, Abingdon, Routledge. DOI:10.4324/9780203357071-35

Hall, S., Critcher, C., Jefferson, T., Clarke, J. and Roberts, B. (1978) *Policing the Crisis: Mugging, the state and law and order*, London, Macmillan Press

Huntington, S. (1993) The clash of civilizations? *Foreign Affairs*. Vol. 72, No. 3 pp 22-49

Huntington, S. (1996) *The clash of civilizations and the remaking of world order*, New York, Simon & Schuster

Ivankova, N., Creswell, J. and Stick, S. (2006) Using mixed-methods sequential explanatory design: From theory to practice, *Field Methods*, Vol. 18, No. 1 pp 3-20

Limbu, B. (2009) Illegible humanity: The refugee, human rights, and the question of representation, *Journal of Refugee Studies*, Vol. 22, No. 3 pp 257-282

Malkki, L. (1996) Speechless emissaries: Refugees, humanitarianism, and dehistoricization, *Cultural Anthropology*, Vol. 11, No. 3 pp 337-404

Manning, P. (2001) *News and news sources: A critical introduction*, London, Sage Publications

Nyers, P. (2006) *Rethinking refugees: Beyond states of emergencies*, New York, Routledge

Rajaram, P. K. (2002) Humanitarianism and representations of the refugee, *Journal of Refugee Studies*, Vol. 15, No. 3 pp 247-264

Santos, R., Roque, S. and Santos, S. (2018) De-securitising 'the South in the North'? Gendered narratives on the refugee flows in the European mediascape, *Contexto Internacional*, Vol. 40, No. 3 pp 453-477

Schlesinger, P. (1990) Rethinking the sociology of journalism, Ferguson, M. (ed.) *Public communication*, London, Sage pp 61-83

Smith, H. (2019) Greece sets out emergency plans to tackle surge of migrant arrivals, *Guardian*, 2 September. Available online at https://www.theguardian.com/world/2019/sep/02/greece-sets-out-emergency-plans-to-tackle-surge-of-migrant-arrivals, accessed on 7 February 2022

Thorbjørnsrud, K. and Figenschou, T. (2014) Do marginalized sources matter? A comparative analysis of irregular migrant voice in Western media, *Journalism Studies*, Vol. 17, No. 3 pp 337-355

UNHCR (2019) Greece: Factsheet, December. Available online at https://data2.unhcr.org/en/documents/details/73592, accessed on 2 February 2021

UNHCR (2020a) Refugee data finder, December. Available online at https://www.unhcr.org/refugee-statistics/, accessed on 2 February 2021

UNHCR (2020b) Europe situations: Data and trends; Arrivals and displaced populations, December. Available online at https://data2.unhcr.org/en/documents/details/84470, accessed on 2 February 2021

UNHCR (2021) Figures at a glance, June. Available online at https://www.unhcr.org/figures-at-a-glance.html, accessed on 2 October 2021

Van Dijk, T. A. (2000) New(s) racism: A discourse analytical approach, Cottle, Simon (ed.) *Ethnic minorities and the media: Changing cultural boundaries*, Buckingham, Open University Press pp 33-49

Wisdorff, F. (2019) Does Frontex need 'invasion competence'? *Die Welt*, 16 September

Zelizer, B. (2004) *Taking journalism seriously: News and the academy*, London, Sage Publications

Zetter, R. (2007) More labels, fewer refugees: Remaking the refugee label in an era of globalization, *Journal of Refugee Studies*, Vol. 20, No. 2 pp 172-192

Interviewees

Aman (2020) Interviewed on 21 April 2020

Amelia (2020) Interviewed 17 April 2020

Benjamin (2020) Interviewed on 15 April 2020

Ella (2020) Interview on 20 April 2020

Emma, (2020) Interviewed on 20 April 2020

John (2020) Interviewed on 27 April 2020

Nabil (2020) Interviewed on 18 April 2020

Olivia (2020) Interviewed on 21 April 2020

Sadia (2020) Interviewed on 30 April 2020

Note on the contributors

Nanna Vedel-Hertz is a Danish journalist specialising in war and conflict and refugees. She is co-founder of aidóni and a senior fellow at Humanity in Action. Her research and work focus on refugees, the importance of sourcing, the intersection between activism and journalism and marginalised groups' access to being heard in the news media. She holds a Master's degree in Journalism, Media and Globalisation. This work was carried out as a part of her MA programme. Her photography of refugees on Lesvos has been exhibited in Copenhagen by the EU.

Dr Allaina Kilby is a lecturer in journalism at Swansea University and is the Programme Director for the Journalism, Media and Communication BA programme. She has a number of papers, chapters and journal articles published in the areas of journalism, political communication, conflict and TV satire. In addition to political communication, her research interests include lifestyle journalism, with a specific focus on sexual and relationship education.

BOOK REVIEWS

Handbook of global media ethics, Vols 1 and 2
Stephen J. A. Ward (ed.)
Springer Nature, Switzerland, 2021 pp 1,460
ISBN 978331932102-8 (hbk);
9783319321035 (ebook)

The 1,460 page (!) *Handbook of global media ethics*, edited by Stephen J. A. Ward and a team of section editors, is now available from Springer Nature (Switzerland) both as a book and ebook. Ward has amazingly assembled a team of seven section editors and seventy-seven authors from many countries and (sub) disciplines including such veteran leaders in the field as Clifford Christians, Kathleen Culver, Ian Richards, Richard Lance Keeble, Wendy Wyatt, Bob Picard, Robert Fortner, Brant Houston, Patrick Plaisance, Linda Steiner, Brian Winston and Herman Wasserman. To this group, dozens of 'rising stars' have been added with wide representation across gender, race and geography.

Each of the seven sections has its own introduction by a section editor and a 'further reading' list. The sections are titled 'Concepts and problems', 'Approaches and methods', 'Digital and social media', 'Global issues for global media', 'Freedom, security, war and global reporting' 'Global ethics and journalism practice' and 'Global media ethics in a geographical framework'. The comprehensive and hyper-scholarly work includes photographs, links, citations and notes – and concludes with a substantial index.

Ward should be particularly congratulated not only for overseeing the editing of more than fourteen hundred pages, but also for recruiting such talent, navigating the rapids with a challenging publisher and for writing seven of the chapters himself. Moreover, he was able to encourage Clifford Christians, undoubtedly the senior and central pillar of the media ethics field, to be his 'right hand' and co-editor throughout the project.

The first US media ethics summit conference, in Massachusetts, in 1987, involved only 20 representatives from organisations and publications. Twenty years later at the second summit, in Tennessee, twice as many organisations and publications were represented. Ward's scope is a reminder of just how widely the field is expanding only fifteen years later.

The volume also reports the overview and outcomes of the largest media ethics project to date by which the United Nations assembled leading experts from all populated continents and provided curricula for students and faculty willing to participate at the college, high school and elementary levels of education. (In the interest of full disclosure, I wrote that chapter and was the UN representative regarding media ethics.)

In my view, every library, communication/journalism department and colleague who teaches media ethics should own a copy of this new reference-cum-textbook and share it with their students. If 'bible' derives from ancient Greek meaning 'books' or 'a book of books', *The handbook of global media ethics* is a new 'bible' for the field complementing the many compilations, anthologies, reference texts and inventories (think Kurian, Gerbner, Jones, Wilkins, Nordenstreng, Christians et al) which preceded it. Congratulations to Stephen Ward, Clifford Christians and their large and impressive team.

Dr Tom Cooper, Emeritus,
Emerson College,
Boston,
Massachusetts

Fall: The mystery of Robert Maxwell
John Preston
Penguin, 2021 pp 344
ISBN: 9780241388686

Robert Maxwell was a media magnate and a media monster. Created by himself and others, destroyed by himself (and others?). At one point his company was in the top ten media businesses in the world. He rubbed shoulders with presidents and prime ministers and had scores of academics in his thrall. Yet his tale ended in tragedy when he fell off (or was pushed from?) the deck of super yacht, the *Lady Ghislaine*, on 4 November 1991. Tributes poured in from political leaders and publishers around the world as he was buried on the Mount of Olives in Jerusalem five days later. It emerged soon after Captain Bob's death that he was a massive fraudster who had stolen hundreds of millions from the pension funds of 'his' newspaper, the *Mirror*, to keep the share price afloat and finance his worldwide acquisitions. Maxwell's life was always a tragedy in waiting.

This is a masterful biography by John Preston. Thoroughly and carefully researched, it follows the successes of his *Very English scandal* and *The dig* – both made into television adaptations. This one will too, especially now that Maxwell's favourite daughter, Ghislaine, is languishing in a US prison for many years following her sex trafficking conviction. Her father avoided that fate by death. Behind he left a trail of financial destruction among his closest family (I live in the same road as did son Kevin, 'the biggest bankrupt in Britain', in Oxford. His former wife still lives here) and worse for tens of thousands of poor pensioners.

How did Maxwell – born poor as Ján Ludvík Hyman Binyamin Hoch in Czechoslovakia in 1923 – achieve such media success? Will-power, hype, bullying and naivety from his clients. Those in the rarefied climes of the academe should never forget that his Pergamon Press empire was based on publishing dubious academic journals especially in Eastern Europe which gave ventilation and space to 'academics'. They were subscribed to by libraries worldwide to provide Maxwell with a solid initial financial foundation. Who now remembers the *Bulgarian Journal of Social Science* apart from the contributors? From this foundation of sand, Maxwell was able to acquire the *Mirror* stable of titles, the *New York Daily News* and much more. He used them all as his personal PR vehicles and his media power to gain more importance and leverage and plunder their assets.

One Maxwell survivor is fellow media magnate Rupert Murdoch. Wherever the two of them locked horns, 'Rupe' came off the winner in Europe and the USA. Murdoch may be as equally unpleasant as Maxwell but he is much more savvy and strategic. Maxwell was all greed and ego. Murdoch does seem to care more about the 'product' even if it is *Fox News*.

Maxwell used his bullying and money to buy some big names to serve him. Peter Jay – then 'the cleverest man in Britain', later the UK ambassador to the USA – was employed as his 'chief of staff': in essence a factotum. Many famous journalistic names from Joe Haines to Alastair Campbell to Roy Greenslade became Maxwell men. They served the master and his myths even, as in Greenslade's case, aiding Maxwell to fix the results of the *Mirror* 'Spot the ball' competition to make it unwinnable. They did it for salary and for the chance to be part of the bubble of hype. Maxwell saw himself as a saviour of British media, politics, the Commonwealth Games, Israel, the world. Those around him were happy to play pliant disciples. In the media worlds then and now nothing succeeds like excess. Maxwell had that in spades with his yacht, private jet and helicopter flitting between his London HQ – which, as only he could, he rebadged as 'Maxwell House' and his 'council house' Headington Hall in Oxford. The worst tale I know is about him getting out of his chopper in London atop the *Mirror* and urinating over the side of the building impervious to the little people on whom it landed below.

Maxwell literally peed on the world, too, using his media power to its fullest. From 'Backing Britain' to lying to colleagues to betraying his wife Betty, constantly, there was always less to him that at first appears. He may have been large in size but not in spirit. I made a short BBC film about Oxford United which he then owned. He tried to bully me the night before on the phone and on the day rearranged the advertising hoardings to catch the BBC camera angles. At the end he came storming out of the directors' box shouting to Ghislaine: 'How did we lose? How did we lose?' They had drawn 1-1 with Everton.

Truth was never a strong point of Cap'n Bob: a home-made Citizen Kane out of the Holocaust with a proud war record. This book, winner of the Costa Prize in 2021, is a cracker. Buy it, read it, pass on to your students. A vital warning from media history for us all.

John Mair, editor of 46 'hackademic' books about the media in the last decade. The latest, *Populism and the media*, was published by Abramis in 2021.

Many different kinds of love: A story of life, death and the NHS
Michael Rosen
Ebury Publishing, 2021 pp 288
ISBN 9781529109450

Every deep-drawn breath: A critical care doctor on healing, recovery, and transforming medicine in the ICU
Wes Ely
Scribner, 2021 pp 352
ISBN 9781922310644

'I am not who I was,' writes Michael Rosen in *Many different kinds of love*. This memoir – composed of prose, verse, journal entries, texts and emails – chronicles a sudden and stormy experience with Covid-19 and a long spell in the liminal space of being on the *edge* of the world of the living but not *quite* in the world of the dead. Rosen, 74, a poet, author and broadcaster, describes his entrée into intensive care:

A doctor is standing by my bed
asking me if I would sign a piece of paper
which would allow them to put me to sleep
and pump air into my lungs.
'Will I wake up?'
'There's a 50:50 chance.'
'If I say no,' I say.
'Zero.'
And I sign.

Wes Ely is at the other end of the stethoscope to Rosen. He is an American intensive care physician, dedicated to achieving better outcomes for patients ventilated and sedated for long periods. He reflects, in *Every deep-drawn breath*, on how increasing survival can mean doing patients harm. Thus, Rosen and Ely's books dovetail, providing a window into the interwoven worlds of the intensivist and patient.

The intensive care unit (ICU) is the place where the ethics of life and death often play out. Families wrestle with the 'wishes', known or not, of their loved ones; doctors decide the point at which further treatment seems futile; define when brain death, the modern marker of the cessation of life, occurs. And, regrettably, doctors must sometimes, in some countries and in some situations, determine the best allocation of limited and expensive care resources.

But for all these complex and fraught discussions, there is very little grappling with the actual lived experience of survivorship in the post-ICU space. Some patients in Ely's book wish they had not been ICU successes and survivors.

The usual metrics of success are the number of patients leaving the ICU bound for a step-down ward, rehabilitation unit or, if very lucky, home – while 'unsuccessful' patients are trolleyed to the mortuary. It is by this exit data that units and individual treatments are evaluated. However, Ely muses that it is the regime of ventilating and sedating patients that is creating noxious sequelae. Delirium is so common an experience for in-patients that psychotropic drug administration is the norm. Profound muscle wasting and weakness commences within only a few days of ventilation and sedation. Large gaps pepper patients' memories. These coalesce to create a toxic aftermath, where patients suffer dire consequences in addition to any fallout from their original diagnoses.

When Ely finally gets talking to survivors, he realises that whilst the ICU experience may be terrifying, the life after ICU may even be worse. Some 50 per cent had depression; 10 per cent are still terrorised by delirium. Most do not return to their usual occupation, and 20 per cent have post-intensive care syndrome (PICS). These ex-patients are not as they were. Survivors with PICS struggled not just with depression, anxiety and post-traumatic stress disorders but with memory loss and cognitive decline as seen with marked changes on their brain scans. After weeks and months of immobility whilst sedated and ventilated, their bodies were unable to perform basic tasks of daily life such as showering, eating and walking. Alive, yes. Living a good life? Probably not.

Ely begins to investigate alternatives to prolonged ventilation and sedation. A simple but effective tool to help ICU patients navigate the lost days, weeks and sometimes months is through a journal. From an idea first expressed by a British nurse-scientist Christina Jones that PTSD decreases markedly when staff write daily entries in a journal for the patient to read later; to make sense of what happened: why and when and how. Our ability to make storied sense out of illness, intensive care and rehabilitation depends on aide-mémoires.

This particular strategy filters through to Rosen's own care, and he includes his ICU journal entries in his book.

And Rosen is living a post-intensive care life where death is not cancelled but postponed; it is a gentler, albeit frustrating life, for his body is not the same; he has lost sight in one eye, has much-diminished hearing and a saggy, weak hammock of a body. Rosen departs ICU but needs to re-learn all the activities of daily living. He must learn to walk again with the aid of Sticky McStickysticky, his cane.

Rosen is writing through his intensive care trauma with this volume (and a children's book with Sticky as the hero) about the long post-Covid, post-ICU road to rehabilitation.

We will all likely have contact with intensive care in our lives; whether at life's beginning, middle or end; as a patient, family member or friend. And as Ely writes, we need care that sends patients home alive and without new brain and body diseases. I wish these two books could talk to each other. Lived-experience accounts could inform professional practice, and together grow a more humane approach to truly patient-centred care.

**Dr Annmaree Watharow,
The Centre for Disability Research and Policy,
University of Sydney**

The Routledge companion to journalism ethics
Lada Trifonova Price, Karen Sanders and Wendy N. Wyatt (eds)
Routledge, Abingdon, Oxon. 2022 pp 513
ISBN: 9780367206475 (hbk);
9781032041599 (pbk); 9780429262708 (ebk)

There cannot be a better time for a book on journalism ethics than this when the media is grappling with issues related to technological advancement, market dynamics, revenue models, power politics, and the after-effects of pandemics. This volume of 513 pages compiled by Lada Trifonova Price, Karen Sanders, and Wendy N. Wyatt brings us 57 diverse chapters on journalism ethics by more than 60 contributors from around the world, engaging with the field at both the macro and micro levels.

The editors started work in 2018 and confronted many disruptions along the way, some predictable, others unexpected. These include the 'existential' crisis in the field of journalism; financial pressures on news and media organisations; continuing digital disruption; increasing levels of mistrust in media; fake news; the suppression of the press; attacks on journalists – and, of course, and the Covid-19 pandemic (p. 1).

They have included and responded to all these issues in this volume. However, while highlighting problems they have also sought to provide solutions. These might be theoretical – in the case Pieter J. Fourie makes for a fundamental reconceptualisation of *journalism* ethics as *communication* ethics to accommodate the postmodern world of digital mediated communication (chapter 3 pp 28-35). Or Tony Harcup's reflection on the principles – and the route to practices – of slow journalism as ethical journalism (chapter 9 pp 77-84). Leyla Tavernaro-Haidarian invites us to explore and adopt the concept of Ubuntu derived from African oral traditions – the notion that 'I am because we are' – in journalism (chapter 11 pp 93-100) and Yayu Feng, in chapter 4, discusses the Confucian approach to journalism ethics (pp 36-44). Svein Brurås highlights the role self-regulation plays in preserving press freedom (chapter 55 pp. 487-495).

The book is divided into four sections, each of which addresses a central theme. The first examines the historical trajectory of journalism ethics, drawing on conceptual approaches and presenting practical perspectives from Brazil, China and Japan. A very suitable start to the journey of the book both academically and professionally. In the first chapter in this section, Karen Sanders emphasises the importance of journalism ethics in these testing times (pp 9-17) and Thomas Hanitzsch offers a compelling argument for the need for further research on ethical ideologies (pp 45-52). Lindsay Palmer draws on post-colonial perspectives to focus on the exploitation of local journalists in poorer nations by Western news organisations (chapter 7, pp 62-68). Herman Wasserman argues for a global approach to media ethics and an ethical way of life embracing an 'ethic of listening' to inform journalism practice (pp.69-76) A further consideration of de-Westernising the field is offered by Saadia Izzeldin Malik in an Islamic perspective on media ethics (chapter 10 pp 85-92). In chapter 12 Nakhi Mishol-Shouli and Oren Golan offer an ethical code of communal journalism, focusing on journalists working in enclave societies: Ultra-Orthodox (Haredi) Jews in Israel and the Amish in the United States (pp 101-109).

The bedrock of section one leads on to a focus in section two on the range of enduring issues in journalism ethics, some global and others highly localised. These concern the broad issues of privacy, public interest, neutrality, balance, objectivity, truth, transparency, professional autonomy, ethical reporting of religion, women, traumatic events, followed by seven case studies from India, Turkey, Russia, Hungary, Slovenia, Spain, and Central and Eastern Europe. These collectively illustrate the status of journalism ethics today in the broader form and in specific cultural, political and social contexts.

The third section of the book addresses emerging areas such as data journalism, user-generated content, artificial intelligence, virtual reality, fake news, native advertising and social media. The ethical issues in these areas are also emerging and these are explored here. Bastiaan Vanacker gives an overview of ethical issues in data journalism (chapter 34, pp 301-309) while Ramon Salaverria analyses ethical concerns in user generated content (UGC) and automated content (chapter 36, pp 319-327) Artificial intelligence (AI), virtual reality (VR) and clickbait are explored at length in chapters 37, 38, and 39 respectively. Kati Tusinski Berg highlights the damage to trust in journalism caused by fake news and suggests some solutions (chapter 43 pp 380-389). The section brings new knowledge and adds value to the existing academic as well as professional knowledge pool.

The last section offers solutions – generic and specific – to the issues and concerns discussed widely in the previous sections. Susanne Fengler addresses self-regulation in an international context (chapter 47, pp 419-426), Katharine Sarikakis and Lisa Winter interrogate journalism's codes of conduct (chapter 48, pp 427-434), while chapters 52, 53, 54, and 56, consider specific cases and contexts in, respectively, the UK, Spain, Western Europe, Bulgaria and Romania. Wendy N. Wyatt draws the book to a close on the teaching praxis of journalism ethics and suggests good practices beyond the classroom for effective teaching (chapter 57, pp 504-512).

As a reviewer, I recommend this book to researchers and students working in media and mass communication for theoretical and empirical guidance.

Archana Kumari,
Assistant Professor,
Department of Mass Communication and New Media,
Central University of Jammu, Bagla (Rahya-Suchani)

ethical space
The International Journal of Communication Ethics

Subscription information
Each volume contains four issues, published quarterly.

Annual Subscription (including postage)

Personal Subscription	Printed	Online
UK	£50	£25
Europe	£60	£25
RoW	£75	£25

Institutional Subscription		
UK	£175	
Europe	£185	
RoW	£200	

Single Issue - Open Access   £300

Enquiries regarding subscriptions and orders should be sent to:

Journals Fulfilment Department
Abramis Academic
ASK House
Northgate Avenue
Bury St Edmunds
Suffolk, IP32 6BB
UK

Tel: +44(0)1284 717884
Email: info@abramis.co.uk

www.ingramcontent.com/pod-product-compliance
Lightning Source LLC
Chambersburg PA
CBHW080847010526
44114CB00017B/2389